D0058407

formatio

TRADITION. EXPERIENCE.
TRANSFORMATION.

Formatio books from InterVarsity Press follow the rich tradition of the church in the journey of spiritual formation. These books are not merely about being informed, but about being transformed by Christ and conformed to his image. Formatio stands in InterVarsity Press's evangelical publishing tradition by integrating God's Word with spiritual practice and by prompting readers to move from inward change to outward witness. InterVarsity Press uses the chambered nautilus for Formatio, a symbol of spiritual formation because of its continual spiral journey outward as it moves from its center. We believe that each of us is made with a deep desire to be in God's presence. Formatio books help us to fulfill our deepest desires and to become our true selves in light of God's grace.

the path of
CELTIC PRAYER
An Ancient Way to Everyday Joy

CALVIN MILLER

IVP Books

An imprint of InterVarsity Press
Downers Grove, Illinois

InterVarsity Press
P.O. Box 1400, Downers Grove, IL 60515-1426
World Wide Web: www.ivpress.com
E-mail: email@ivpress.com

InterVarsity Press® is the book-publishing division of InterVarsity Christian Fellowship/USA®, a student movement active on campus at hundreds of universities, colleges and schools of nursing in the United States of America, and a member movement of the International Fellowship of Evangelical Students. For information about local and regional activities, write Public Relations Dept., InterVarsity Christian Fellowship/USA, 6400 Schroeder Rd., P.O. Box 7895, Madison, WI 53707-7895, or visit the IVCF website at <www.intervarsity.org>.

All Scripture quotations, unless otherwise indicated, are taken from the Holy Bible, New International Version®. NIV®. Copyright ©1973, 1978, 1984 by International Bible Society. Used by permission of Zondervan Publishing House. All rights reserved.

Excerpts from Where Three Streams Meet *by Seán Ó Duinn, ©2000 is used by permission of Columba Press.*

Excerpts from Journeys on the Edges *by Thomas O'Loughlin (New York: Orbis, 2000) are reprinted with permission of Orbis Books and Darton, Longman and Todd.*

Excerpts from Celtic Spirituality *by Oliver Davies, ©1999 by Oliver Davies, Paulist Press, Inc., New York, Mahwah, N.J. Used with permission. www.paulistpress.com*

Excerpts from A Welsh Pilgrim's Manual *by Brendan O'Malley (Gomer Press, 1989) are reprinted with permission of Gomer Press.*

Every effort has been made to contact copyright holders for materials quoted in this book. The author will be pleased to rectify any omissions in future editions if notified by copyright holders.

Design: Cindy Kiple

Images: boardwalk: Nikolaevich/Getty Images
paper: istockphoto.com

ISBN 978-0-8308-3504-1

Printed in the United States of America ∞

Library of Congress Cataloging-in-Publication Data

Miller, Calvin.
   The path of Celtic prayer: an ancient way to contemporary joy/
   Calvin Miller.
     p. cm.
   Includes bibliographical references.
   ISBN 978-0-8308-3504-1 (cloth: alk. paper)
   1. Prayer—Christianity. 2. Spirituality—Celtic Church. 3.
   Celts—Religion. 4. Christianity—Celtic influences. I. Title.
   BV210.3.M55 2007
   248.3'2089916—dc22

                           2007011181

P	20	19	18	17	16	15	14	13	12	11	10	9	8	7	6	5	4	3	2
Y	23	22	21	20	19	18	17	16	15	14	13	12	11		10	09	08	07	

CONTENTS

TO THE READER

I am not a groupie. I am not a celebrant of any new form of "hula-hoop" theology. I did not take up my current interest in Celtic theology because it has achieved a popular fascination. It's just that something happened to my worldview when I stood on the decks of a ferry crossing from Oban to the Isle of Iona. Call it romantic nonsense if you will, but there are epiphany moments, in which new revelations seem to summon us from a contentment with who we are to new spiritual adventures. These epiphanies enable us to cast off our dull religious comforts in favor of a riskier pilgrimage.

As I stood there surveying Iona, I asked myself, *Why in the name of all that is Oklahoma in my origin was I on the rough waters that separate endless islands of the Hebrides archipelago?* So I opened up to the possibilities that I was not through learning all about prayer that God wanted me to know.

In the distance across the waters, I could see the Abbey of Iona, not a notable structure when compared with the great cathedrals of Europe, but the late medieval vestige of people who had lived on the island a thousand years before and, who in talking with God in the wild wind and sea, had formed a view of God that sent missionaries around the known world. This fire that burned in the century after Rome had burned was a flame fueled by an ardor that most Western Christians have never known. I wanted to find the flame again. For it is sometimes by looking at the past that the present amends its dead soul, and there dawns a hope that the future will be born with new vitality.

I have since learned I am not alone in the quest.

This book is not a history or cultural examination of the Celts but a book on prayer. From my limited studies of the Celts, I have discovered certain practices and ideas that have enhanced my worship and prayer life. In this book, I hope to offer you some aspects of Celtic spiritual practices as a springboard that might enable your prayer life to reach new heights.

GETTING TO KNOW THE CELTS

Celts have often been called the first Europeans or European aborigines. The word *Celt* is from the Greek (*keltos*) and can be translated "alien" or "stranger." Exactly when or where the Celts came from has fostered a long anthropological debate. Some scholars place their beginnings as far back as 1500 B.C. Others say they came from no further back than 500 B.C. Some believe they had their origin in the regions north of India, while others think they were middle European. Whatever their origin, the Celts have come slowly into our awareness with the advance of archaeology. In the centuries before Christ they seem to have been workers in and perhaps owners of Austrian salt mines. We know for sure that Celtic tribes were in England long before the Saxon and Angles arrived to give it the modern name of "Angle Land" or England.

Julius Caesar fought with the Celts (or Gauls, as they were called on the continent) and bragged about killing over one million of them in his attempt to Romanize the barbarians on the northern frontier of his expanding empire. Although we are not sure, it is possible that later Romanization drove the Celts into what is now modern England, Scotland and Wales, and then finally to Ireland.

Seán Ó Duinn, my favorite Celtic scholar and a Benedictine monk, speaks Gaelic (a Celtic tongue) and is as authentic and home grown as Celtic scholars come. Of his Irish heritage he says:

> The remains of this once great civilization, which at its height could be felt as a presence in areas reaching from Ireland to Asia Minor, is now reduced to a tiny remnant in six areas of Western Europe—Brittany, Wales, Cornwall, Scotland, Isle of Mann, Ireland. The Celtic languages still linger on but only as a whisper. In view of the mighty power of Anglo-American culture, it is surprising that Irish and Welsh are still spoken even in such sadly reduced circumstances. It is surely a sign of their tenacity and vigor in the face of such appalling odds.
>
> While death beckons menacingly at the once great civilization, a lingering breath still remains which perhaps could be the breath of life for the jaded victims of the consumer society. For myth is the great strength of the Celts and myth is associated with the hidden powers of renewal.

By "myth" Ó Duinn really means the mystical soul of Ireland, a heritage that is bringing new insight into genuine spirituality for many Christians.

In Ireland these ancient people met the missionary Patrick, whose evangelistic zeal led thousands of Celts to faith in Christ. There are many popular books that discuss the historical aspects of Patrick's missionary crusade. These books include Thomas Cahill's *How the Irish Saved Civilization* (see also Timothy Joyce's *Celtic Christianity*, Paulist Press's *Celtic Spirituality*, and Philip Freeman's *St. Patrick of Ireland*). It may be that the subjects I cover in this book will increase your own hunger to understand the Celtic ways. If so, I will be more than satisfied to have stirred you to consider this new way of bringing vitality to your walk with Christ.

I have written this book for two reasons. First, I want to address the way the Celtic people related to God to keep their devotion centered on the Savior. But I also want to demonstrate how these ancient lovers of God were able to strip away institutional business and empty religiosity that can separate Christians from Christ.

Many Christians suffer from historical nearsightedness. They seem to believe that all real spiritual vitality began with the Reformation or with the Great Awakening or with Charles Haddon Spurgeon. And yet all through history there have been great men and women of God who loved Christ and pursued an ever-deepening relationship with him. It is wholly reasonable to seek among these brothers and sisters of ours a spiritual vitality and a way of life that we seem to have mislaid. Celtic spirituality may be able to breathe its "right now" life into our feeble discipleship.

Within this book I present six principles of prayer I have put to work in my life. I hope that they may be put to work in your life as well. Then Christ will find a living center of praise within the both of us.

The Stowe Missal (an ancient prayer book) was written some-time between A.D. 790 and 820. It is not Celtic in its origin but is Celtic at its heart. If in these pages I can bring you toward the God of the *Stowe Missal,* we will both find much that we need to bring us into conformity in Christ. The missal calls to us in this way.

> Father, all powerful and ever-living God,
> we do well always and everywhere to give you thanks
> through Jesus Christ our Lord.
> You (O Father), with your only begotten Son and the
> Holy Spirit are God.
> (You are) God, one and immortal;
> (You are) God, incorruptible and unmoving;
> (You are) God, invisible and faithful;
> (You are) God, wonderful and worthy of praise;
> (You are) God, strong and worthy of honour;
> (You are) God, most high and magnificent;
> (You are) God, living and true;
>
> We believe you;
> We bless you;
> We adore you;
> And we praise your name forever more.
>
> (We praise you) through (Christ) who is the salvation of
>   the universe;
> through (Christ) who is the life of human beings;
> through (Christ) who is the resurrection of the dead.
>
> Through him the angels praise your majesty;
> the dominations adore;

the powers of the heaven of heavens tremble;
the virtues and the blessed seraphim concelebrate in
    exultation;
so grant, we pray you, that our voices may be admitted
to that chorus, in humble declaration of your glory;

I invite you therefore to walk with me by the glow of an old
lamp whose light burns new in this generation.

Calvin Miller

God shall not
refuse or reject
whoever strives to praise Him
at the beginning and end
of the day.

A WELSH POEM

In my study of the years following the heroic age of the beginnings of Celtic Chris-tianity I discovered that while some characteristics and practices did change, many of the original features of Celtic Christianity endured.... [T]he basic vision endured: creation is graced by God and by the immanence of this God; creation is filled with God's presence and with the presence of those who have died and are now in the bosom of God. The Celtic propensity for intense religious longing endured. A mythic and imaginative stance toward the world continued to be expressed in the great outpour-ing of literature and art.... No matter how things were changing around them, how-ever, there were still many people living an intense Christian and Holy life.

TIMOTHY JOYCE

INTRODUCTION

Human beings are innate believers. While agnostics are sometimes celebrated for their unsure notions about God, atheism isn't likely to take hold in any permanent way. Why? Because we are so needy, helpless and insecure that we remain obsessed with something or Someone greater than ourselves. Not only are we needy, we hurry our lives deathward in a dead heat with that great universal clock that is destined to outrun us. We live face to face with our temporariness. And while we are trapped in the busy, empty *now*, we are convinced there must be—or must have been—a day when God seemed nearer and more accessible.

Our discontentment with our present affairs keeps us looking backward, hungering for times in our lives when we experienced God as clearly present. Even our casual reading tastes have found us out. The recent rash of novels about Christ's second coming may be popular because they hold forth a kind of promise that when Jesus comes again, all the pain of our empty age will be swallowed up in the warm presence of God. But at the foundation of such hope lies a reality much greater than current popular fiction. We—at least in our searching moments—want Jesus to come again. Why? We are eager for union with Christ. The second coming promises an end to our roller-coaster relationship with God.

Yes, we are inebriated with a yearning after God. We are like earthly junkies needing our "God fix" to live. "The Celt was very much a God-intoxicated man," says John McQuarrie. This narcotic state of heart is indeed intoxicating. For when we have drunk deeply of the nature of God, there is born within us a God thirst that can never be slaked by any lesser stream. The Celts of the sixth century also believed that Jesus was coming soon, and their expectation of the second coming created a faith of great vitality.

> While later Christians in the Celtic lands did not follow Patrick in viewing the end as imminent, they did believe they were living in the final times. This is what Adomnán wrote in the preface to his *Vita Columbae:* "In these final times of the earth, (Columba's) name shall be a light to the oceanic island-provinces." Slightly later an anonymous Irish preacher wrote: "Our Lord Jesus Christ has announced this to us . . . that the end of this world is coming closer every day. . . . I hope his coming will be in the very near future and that he will judge the whole universe with fire" (*In nomine Dei summi*, homily 2). This is an alien notion to Christians today, for we think of time as just rolling on, day after day, and while we may measure time as "AD" all this means is that we are using a Christian (or convenient) reckoning system; we no longer place the emphasis where these Celtic writers did, on "the year *of the Lord*."

Our failure to perceive Christ's imminent return as our "blessed hope" (Titus 2:13) has contributed to our feelings of separateness from God. The problem is not so much that we seldom think about his coming but that we are no longer excited by the prospect. Paul says there is a crown laid up for all those who love his appearing (2 Timothy 4:8). But do we love and anticipate his appearing? What of our blasé contentment with things as they are, Christless and self-managed? Many of us are secular captives, separated from God and content with the divorce.

This book proposes a kind of prayer that can end our amputated feelings of separateness from God. I believe that God's seeming remoteness can be partially healed by looking backward to a distant, vital day. Long ago when the Celts built their own rustic kingdom of God in what would later be the British Isles, their fervor in prayer washed their world in a vital revival.

The Celts found God no casual diversion. They were too needy to talk about spiritual things over tea cups and pastries. As with much of Europe, the world was always falling down around them. Infant mortality was as high as life was short. Leprosy was common. The plague, pandemic. Medicine was unknown and hospitals were centuries in the future. Their todays were unsteady and their tomorrows obscure.

In desperate times, living becomes an altar where you pray and sing because the only good news of the day is that God lives longer than you do. And God promises you that even if your days are few, your dying is not a wall, but a set of gates. Beyond this portal lies a reason to esteem your life. God stirs the ashes of your old hopes when you have faced the fact that your lifespan, like that of the Celts, is short. But your prayers endure forever. None of them die. They live in the air about us and they move us like the breeze of Pentecost. They may appear dead, but they sometimes lay like an ember in the dull, gray ash of the present moment. Then the Spirit blows, the coals flare and the fire burns hot. Even now, the Celtic embers of spirituality are catching fire all around us.

But a blazing church is not what most people find when they go to a typical worship service today. Disinterest, sparse attendance, boredom: these are more common perceptions. British writer Ian Smith berated the church for its lack of spiritual vitality:

> When little is demanded from members, little is given. If commitment requires no more than occasional attendance at Communion, it is not surprising that the average level of participation among members is low. There are large numbers who belong and believe, but contribute very little. In order to grow—indeed, just to stand still—it is essential that the church starts to tap and to mobilize these underutilized resources. The important thing is not only regular attendance at worship but involvement in church activities during the week. How can this level of commitment be achieved? The answer lies in inverting the first principle: when much is demanded from members, much is given.

Such spiritual lethargy was not the nature of Celtic trust. Vitality—flame and gale—was the heart of the Celtic faith. This is both the practice and the hope of all that is being born in current Celtic revival. Early in the fifth century Patrick (c. 390-c. 460) brought a living faith from Britain to Ireland, then in the sixth century Columba (c. 521-597) brought it to Scotland. These two rustic missionaries were like a spiritual wind, driving its warm advance across a cold and Christless world. From the Spirit's breath a new kind of worship is once again rising out of ancient devotion. The Celtic way born long ago in the cold, dank Hebrides Islands stirs anew.

THE CELTIC FORMS OF PRAYER

The Celts' way of devotion was so rich and varied that it is foolhardy to limit them to a mere six types of prayer. Yet this is precisely what I want to do—in order to allow us to get some practical handles on their devotion. Thinking of it in this limited way will allow us to grasp the significant aspects of their devotion that are transferable to our age.

The Celts prayed in ways that were most natural and contextual in their society. Like all "unmissionized" people, the Celts were not just idly waiting for someone to bring them a theology. When the first missionaries arrived, the Celts had their own pantheon and natural theologies. They, like Israel in Exodus with its Baals and icons, lived outside a lot. They worshiped their own gods they had drawn from the natural world. Because nature is too vast for humans to grasp, the pre-Christian Celts looked to the gods of sea and forest for help. They thought these outdoor deities could be manipulated with prayers and incantations. A dry cow, a sick sheep, a toxic well, a fevered child, the advance of plague: all of these things had to be dealt with. So they appealed to their pantheon of gods with songs and prayers and incantations that they believed would bend divine favor in their direction.

Into this mix of nature and faith, the good news of Christ,

brought by Patrick and Columba, swelled like new music among the natives of Ireland and Scotland. Patrick and Columba were saints in the best sense of the word. We sometimes get the feeling that saints are heavenly minded Christians who fast and pray until they are interrupted by someone needing a miracle. After performing the miracle, they go right back to praying. But in truth, Patrick and Columba were pastors in touch with the communities they served. They lived among the unconverted and preached evangelistically. They shaped their cultures with the passion of Christ's original apostles.

When Patrick, Columba and other Christian missionaries brought the gospel to Ireland and Scotland, the Celts ceased being insecure pagans and became secure Christians. And because they remained rural peoples, they came to see the Christian God as the King of nature. Having made the world and all that was in it, God had displayed himself in every aspect of his creation. This invocation typifies Celtic devotion:

> Thou King of the Moon
> Thou King of the Sun
> Thou King of the Planets
> Thou King of the Stars
> Thou King of the Globe
> Thou King of the Sky
> Oh! Lovely thy Countenance
> Thou Beauteous Beam

Celtic spirituality is filled with nature runes (poems or incantations) extolling the virtues of the triune God as he fills the natural world. The Celts sometimes struggled not to confuse God and nature; God is always greater than and separate from his creation. Nonetheless, we have much to learn from the way in which they allowed nature to inform their spirituality. For example, in this rune, we see Jesus, who they understood as being one with the Father, as the "Lightener of the Stars."

> Behold the Lightener of the Stars
> On the crests of the clouds,
> And the choralists of the sky
> Lauding Him.
> Coming down with acclaim
> From the Father above,
> Harp and lyre of song
> Sounding to Him.

SIX FORMS OF PRAYER

At the heart of Celtic devotion was a force called the *neart* (sometimes spelled *nirt*). The *neart* was the spiritual energy behind all living things. "In St. Patrick's Breastplate [an ancient Celtic prayer], the person rises up and binds himself with the *neart* or creative power coming from the Trinity, from the acts of Christ's life, from the angels and saints and from the elements—the forces of nature: sky, sun, moon, earth, sea, rock." When we pray to the triune God, we tap into the *neart*. In our pursuit of this spiritual energy, this power of passion, we will examine the following six forms of Celtic prayer.

1. Trinity praying. God, for the Celts, is always triune—the Three-in-One—and they served this great paradox well. They never allowed the Father and the Son and the Spirit to become separate. Celts thought of God as "the three of my love." While they held an adoring view of the Trinity, their perception was never became either too syrupy or too formal. A strong trinitarian formula pervades the whole of Christian Celtic literature. Consider this simple prayer for grace:

> I am bending my knee
> In the eye of the Father who created me,
> In the eye of the Son who died for me,
> In the eye of the Spirit who cleansed me.

This inclusion is an example of what I call "Trinity praying." It entails praying to the full Godhead. Generally speaking, the God who creates and pervades the natural world is never separate from the Son who redeems, nor the Spirit who indwells each believer.

The Trinity, for the Celts, orders all of life and pervades all of nature. The triune God, for the Celts, was not so austere or grand he couldn't take care of ordinary concerns. There are many runes and prayers that these ancients recited to free themselves of daily aches and pains. One of these many trinitarian prayers was for clearing a mote from one's eye:

> In name of Father,
> In name of Son,
> In name of Spirit.
>
> Triune, all alike in might holy,
> Triune, all alike in power of wondrous works,
> Triune, all alike in righteousness and love.
>
> My trust is in the Being of life.
> The mote that is in the blind eye,
> That the true King of my devotion,
> Will gently place it hither on my tongue.

The Celts also prayed to the Trinity to protect them from the slurs of speech by which others directed their venom of hate toward them, and another prayer to the Trinity to protect a newborn babe from epilepsy:

> In the name of Father,
> In the name of Son
> In the name of Spirit,
> Three just and holy.

While they prayed, they wound a straw rope around the baby's body three times. Then the rope was cut into three equal lengths. On and on go these prayers offered to chart the simple course of everyday life. No need was too miniscule for the Trinity to help with.

In looking at their trinitarian entreaties, we might wonder at their naive simplicity in calling all of heaven to meet their need. But they did not see such praying as unreasonable. Simple or not, there was something beautiful in their utter dependency on God. He was, after all, their Creator, Redeemer and Sustainer, and definitely on their side in every issue of life.

2. *Praying the Scriptures.* The Celts took seriously the form of prayer later called "praying the Scriptures." Their fondness for the natural world led them to focus on the Psalms. And their huge optimism led them to a stance of continual gratitude as they prayed. The Psalms' celebration of nature were for the Celts, as they are for all of us, a rich form of praise and thanksgiving. So Celts would open their hearts and pray the Psalms in celebration of their natural world.

The Celts believed that the mere recitation of Scripture held a kind of power. For instance, Psalm 119, which the Celts called *Biáit* (also called the *Beati*) had such efficacy that the Celts believed it should be memorized and recited at any point of need. When recited aloud, this psalm had great power to heal or deliver. Many of the psalms contained healing force, and they were used to drive out demons or disease, as well as to draw themselves closer to God.

Though Psalm 119 was their favorite prayer of power, they also believed the Gospels were special. The words of Christ could be summoned into the arena of prayer with the anticipation of deliverance. Thus, an intimate knowledge of the Gospels was the lifelong pursuit of the Celtic monks of Iona, who copied the Book of Kells. Their painstaking and ornate illumination of the Gospels reveals the special place the Word held in their walk of faith. There is but a thin line that separates the devotional reading of and the praying of Scriptures. When the heart adores Christ as it reads the Bible, it transcends the act of repeating mere words. When we read the Bible while fixed on Christ, it becomes an act of adoration. Our reading then becomes *prayer*.

3. Creature praise. The natural world was the only world the ancients Celts knew. We sometimes leave our enclosed world (houses, cars, offices, stores, churches) and go "camping." But the Celts weren't camping, they lived in nature. They lived with and prayed to and worshiped a God who surrounded them as truly as the fresh air of their green world did. Their intense and natural devotion suggests that the closer we are to nature, the more apt we are to pray and the more fervent our prayers will become. Look, for example, at Israel in Sinai. Their outdoor sojourn revealed YHWH as the "breath" God of the storms, whose wind (*ruach*) created and threatened, and gave life to these trembling, rag-tag Jewish pilgrims. The glorious words of Psalm

19 or Job 37 make it clear that YHWH was not just a fixed temple icon who hid out in a gilded inner sanctum, his "cushy" holy of holies. God could be found among rocks and in bushes. His indisputable power was demonstrated in cobras and earthquakes, hail and fire, quail and tamarack. To some degree the God of the exodus tabernacle—a portable temple—was the God of the Celts. He was the outdoor Almighty who rubbed against the world where the world could best feel the rubbing—outside.

The Celts added up all the attributes of God as depicted in Scripture and prayed to all aspects of his triune being. Neither God's oneness nor his threeness was ever in doubt. Nor was this paradox troubling to them; its ambiguity was welcome in their creature praise; its mystery was the substance of their worship.

4. Long, wandering prayer. Another special form of Celtic devotion is "long, wandering prayer." This kind of prayer characterized the devotional exile and pilgrimages of Celtic monks. These missionaries were called the "peregrini," wandering pilgrims who journeyed not to particular shrines or destinations. They spent their lives in worship and ministry as exiles and aliens and strangers. They prayed as they journeyed, always thanking God for the day and asking him to reveal his will for the land on which they traversed. Coupling prayer with trekking, they partook in what today's pilgrims might call "prayer walking."

Though the travels of Brendan and his "Sanctinauts" in the tales of *Navigatio Sancti Brendani* seems more like myth than real prayer-journeying, the fanciful account reveals the huge missionary imperatives that define the zeal of the peregrini. They made journeys of prayer throughout strange seas and lands. In prayer, they advanced in trust to serve the living God. Regarding these travelers, Hugh Connolly wrote:

> The Celtic image of pilgrimage affords a vision of the Christian life wherein the individual will inevitably encounter suffering and sin, but where he also has the means, through penance, to cleave to that graced process, whereby he is freed from the un-Christ-like elements which impede the growth of his humanity into the kingdom.

So these fantastic voyages should not be taken lightly. Their little coracles (boats) were driven by the breath of the Holy Spirit. They were missionaries who went abroad for "the love of Christ." They journeyed in prayer, and the open sea was their highway to obedience. Sea captains and their crews recited litanies to each other. Their ships were small, and the waters of what we would later call the North Atlantic were perilous. So these peregrini chanted their cries for protection.

"Blest be the boat!" cried the pilot.
"May God the Father bless her!" cried the crew. . . . "Ever eternally."

Only after this liturgy, prayed as often by rough seamen as priests, was the journey undertaken. Religion and prayer were not the special venues of religious professionals. Everyone knew and used the rituals of the holy life, whether or not the culture saw them as holy men and women.

In their travels, the peregrini turned very naturally to ministry. Mother Teresa of Calcutta said that we must never keep our hands so folded in prayer that we refuse to open them to do Christ's service; so it was with the peregrini. They were monks who had said goodbye to the cloister and set sail to pray and minister. They went for God and they went with God. They used their never-ending prayer pilgrimage as a mission to redeem the world and thus enjoyed God's never-ending presence.

5. The lorica. The *lorica* is a breastplate. The prayers that the Celts dubbed by this name were used to call on God to protect the petitioner with grace. The breastplate as Paul describes it in Ephesians 6 is as near a definition of the Celtic armor as one might get. The Celts lived in an insecure world where children died in infancy and the life expectancy was about thirty. They were not reticent to ask God to safeguard their health. It was for his service they existed. So they turned to God to protect them, and their prayers were called the *loricae* (plural).

The blessing we offer others—for birth, life and occupation—will make our life complete until we pray our final prayer. This continuing confession will eventually lead us to bless our death. Our dying is after all the final set of gates that brings to an end—as well as a beginning—our lifelong conversation with the Keeper. The following is a Celtic "death blessing" that was offered over those who lived a fulfilled life:

> God, omit not this woman from Thy covenant,
> And the many evils which she in the body committed,
> That she this night cannot enumerate
> The many evils that she in the body committed
> That she cannot this night enumerate.

> Be this soul on Thine own arm, O Christ,
> Thou King of the City of Heaven,
> And since Thine it was, O Christ, to buy the soul,

At the time of the balancing of the beam,
At the time of the bringing in the judgment,
Be it now on Thine own right hand,
Oh! On Thine own right hand.

And be the holy Michael, king of angels,
Coming to meet the soul,
And leading it home
To the heaven of the Son of God
    The Holy Michael, high king of angels,
    Coming to meet the soul,
    And leading it home
    To the heaven of the Son of God.

6. The confession. The final Celtic prayer we will consider is
the confession. Strictly speaking St. Patrick's *Confession,* the
most famous of all Celtic confessions, is not a prayer. These
confessions really are an account of the spiritual pilgrimage of
the confessor and are often more of a *vita,* a "life," of the confessor. Still, the ancient confessions settle on us as a force of the
Spirit, and their impact stirs us to write and then pray a confession of our own.

The prayer of every confessor centers in on coming to Christ
and the power of that transformation. This is, of course, often
the noblest and highest work of prayer—to come into the presence of God, begging his forgiveness as we seek to own his enduring love. Such confession brings us face to face with God,
and then our forgiven status rushes forward to a celebration
point. So the confession stands very close to the beginning of
our prayer life, but it is also the ongoing conversation that constantly renews our experience.

Patrick's confession reveals his dependence on and close union with Christ:

> I Patrick, a sinner, a most simple countryman, the least of all the faithful and the most contemptable to many, had for father the deacon Calpurnius, . . . he had a small villa where I was taken captive. . . . And the Lord brought down on us the fury of His being and scattered us among many nations. . . . And there the Lord opened my mind to an awareness of my unbelief in order that even so late, I might remember my transgressions and turn with all my heart to the Lord my God.

ENLARGING YOUR WORLD

The forms of prayer at the focus of this book should not be seen as wholly individual and separate. They are found together in almost every instance of my devotion. Thus you will see all of these forms of prayer winding through each chapter. The prayer exercises at the end of each chapter will demonstrate how effective they become when they are used together.

These six forms of prayer will enlarge your world as you walk with Christ. But there is one final aim you should seek in these exercises: union with Christ. Here lies the ultimate spiritual goal of the believer. Hunger for Christ keeps us talking to God till our separation is swallowed up in our unending togetherness with him. Till this union is complete, he who keeps our prayers awaits our union. After all, God hungers for union with us even more than we desire union with him. And prayer is the rails on which our two desires move toward each other. Our devotion moves us from separateness into oneness with God, and the resulting joy is worth the journey.

I want you to understand that the discipline of prayer—vital and deep prayer—though sometimes arduous, does not always remain so. As our love affair with God deepens, our romance with the Trinity will become even more satisfying than mere human romance might be. As we learn to live forever in God's presence, our prayer achieves a lightness of being.

The following Celtic prayer reveals a woman who has just risen in joy to rebuild her fire, praying even as she stirs the gray ashes of the night before and looks for the bright embers of warmth. Though she prays in the presence of all angels, she names only two, archangels Airil and Uiril (customarily spelled *Ariel* and *Uriel*). But she craves more than the presence of the angels, she hungers for the presence of God.

> I will build up my fire today in the presence of the holy angels of heaven, in the presence of Airil of most beautiful form, in the presence of Uiril of all beauty without hate, without envy, without rivalry, without fear, without horror of anyone under the sun, for I have the holy Son of God as my sanctuary. O God, enkindle in my inmost heart the flaming spark of love for my enemy, for my relative, for my friends, for the wise person, for the foolish person, for the unfortunate person, O son of gentle, shining Mary, from the lowest most perverse person to the one of highest fame.

May the simple tasks that occupy our current day provide for us such a matrix for devotion.

God is within Himself a sweet society.

ANSELM

The love and affection of the angels be to you,
The love and affection of the saints be to you,
The love and affection of heaven be to you,
To guard and cherish you.
May God shield you on every steep,
May Christ aid you on every path,
May Spirit fill you on every slope,
On hill and on plain.
May the King shield you in the valleys,
May Christ aid you on the mountains,
May Spirit bathe you on the slopes,
In hollow, on hill, on plain,
Mountain, valley and plain.

FROM THE CARMINA GADELICA

I

TRINITY PRAYER

The Art of Loving All of God

Patrick, it is said, once picked up a shamrock, and noticing that it was a single leaf with three distinct bracts, endowed the Celts with a strong trinitarianism they were never able to shake. Both Protestants and Catholics, of course, accept Patrick's view of the triune God. But while most Christians accept this paradox as the center of our faith, we still have acquired the habit of praying to only one person of the Trinity at a time.

It is almost as though we are trying to alleviate the Almighty's work load by delegating our needs to one person of the Trinity. We generally thank God the Father for the big stuff: sunrise, rainfall and the Rocky Mountains. We are also prone to ask him to protect us from the devastating "acts of God" that mess with our views of his lovingkindness and providential protection. Hurricanes, earthquakes and the like seem to be more the Father's province, and so we generally talk to him to amend the weather, stop the Asian flu or feed the hordes of starving people.

To Jesus we delegate the personal work of our own affairs. Healing, improving our income, stopping our toothache or giving us our daily bread: these are things that Jesus takes care of. This, we unconsciously assume, is compassionate in our thinking, for it saves God the Father from piddling with our petty needs. We see Jesus as far less austere and far more approachable than the Father. We would never sing *What a Friend We Have in God*. Jesus is our friend. He takes care of our intimate needs and bears our heavy burdens "upstairs" where the Father can take care of them.

Finally, the Holy Spirit generally gets slighted in our prayers. He's so invisible that we have no fixed mental image of him, unlike the Father and Son. God, to many, is Grandfather Zeus, powerful and to be feared. He thunders around the ceiling of the Sistine Chapel and keeps a comfortable distance from trembling and weak humans. Jesus is on the wall of the Chapel and a lot closer to the floor, where we live. Even though he is generally friendly with children and widows, he still wears a toga and looks Romanesque.

But what does the Spirit look like? He's invisible—amorphous and cellophane. He may indwell us, but it rarely occurs to us to pray to him. At best he is just a supporting actor in the divine drama. The Holy Spirit is nice, and sometimes he makes us feel good in church, but we rarely have conversations with him. Jesus takes care of our personal stuff. God takes care of the Grand Canyon. And the Holy Spirit gets honorable mention at Communion and baptisms.

The Celts could see one thing most clearly: all humans are born to be the children of God, who is Father of all who call on him in prayer. His triune majesty should always remind us that he is greater than we are, but his regal ownership of our lives should never be allowed to crush us into silence. Here is the most amazing feature of grace: although God has no need of us, being complete within himself, he earnestly desires that we be on speaking terms with him. If Jesus and the Holy Spirit are both God like the Father is, wouldn't it make sense for us to talk to all three as one God when we pray. God is not just one or three: he is the Three-in-One.

But how did the Celts do it? How did they go about praying in this simple way?

THE TRINITY IN CELTIC PRAYER

For Celts, to know God was to talk to him as he is. When they sang or prayed or hunted or played, they did so in the presence of the Father, Son and Holy Spirit. Look, for example, at a typical morning prayer:

I awake in the name of the Father who made me.
I arise in the name of the Son who died to save me:
I rise to greet the dawn in the name of the Spirit who fills me with life.

Their evening prayers read the same way!

I lay me down in the love of my Father.
I surrender my body to rest in the love of my Savior.
I trust my life in sleep to the Spirit who fills me with life.

This consistent adoration of the triune God characterizes Celtic devotion. The Trinity, with all its various symbols, filled their theologies, and the oneness of the three permeated their art. It is doubtful that Patrick ever used a shamrock as an illustration of the Trinity, but Celtic crosses (and other artwork), with their abstract geometric designs, symbolize God's threeness as well as his never-ending sovereignty as the one God. This dramatic form of Celtic art speaks to their holistic view of God.

The primary reason the Celts focused on the Trinity was their own sense that the one God is manifested in plural majesty. Yet their prayers remained simple and to the point. They prayed with a delightful assumption: God, however great he may be, cared about their lives. Theirs was a common life filled with ordinary outdoor tasks and farm chores. Hens needed to be set, sheep needed to be sheared, butter needed to be churned and every task had a proper blessing to make sure that what was done was seen as the gift of God. If their cows went dry, the triune God cared. When a lamb was born dead, it upset the whole pleasure of God. So when the Celts walked with a bold confidence into the presence of God they put the whole Trinity on alert when they had a specific need.

The Creator, the Redeemer, and the empowering Spirit are inseparably one. Let us pray therefore to all three—Father, Son and Spirit—during our morning prayers. This prayer was first written in 1866, but reaches back in spirit to the dim ages of Celtic worship.

> I am bending my knee
> In the eye of the Father who created me,
> In the eye of the Son who purchased me,
> In the eye of the Spirit who cleansed me,
> In friendship and affection.
> Through Thine own Anointed One, O God,
> Bestow upon us fullness in our need.

Notice that in this prayer the worshiper honors the Trinity but concludes the prayer with God's "Anointed One." Surely this is the richest of all ways to pray. The Trinity is honored, and Jesus' name blesses the prayer with a glorious and redemptive finality.

This rich expression in the prayer above can be repeated at noontide. If it was used as a table grace it lacks only specific mention of "the hands that prepared it." It focuses on the Trinity and the triune blessing of the three-personed God. While "at bread," the Celts were greatly enriched by seeing the fullness of God's blessing.

> I am bending my knee
> In the eye of the Father who created me,
> In the eye of the Son who died for me,
> In the eye of the Spirit who cleansed me,
> In love and desire.
> Pour down upon us from heaven
> The rich blessing of Thy forgiveness;
> Thou who art uppermost in the City,
> Be Thou patient with us.
> Grant to us, Thou Saviour of Glory,
> The fear of God, the love of God, and His affection,
> And the will of God to do on earth at all times
> As angels and saints do in heaven;
> Each day and night give us Thy peace.
> Each day and night give us Thy peace.

And let us learn from the example of these early disciples. Let us also go to him at eventide. Let us make Trinity praying our daily art. Let us entreat the great Three-in-One God to bless our rising up and our lying down. Let us surrender ourselves to him as we sleep, for he is ever awake to care for us.

It was customary for ancient peoples to notice the similarities between sleep and death. (The Bible is full of such references.) Some who fell asleep never awoke. And some ancients believed the soul could be sucked out by demons in the night, and the person would never rise again. This fear lives in the child's prayer "If I should die before I wake; I pray the Lord my soul to take." The Celts last waking thoughts before falling asleep were to put the triune God in charge and trust him for safety through the night. They were not terrorized by death, but they did love their homeland and preferred to wake up in the same land where they had gone to bed, and they might well have prayed in the style of the *Carmina Gadelica,*

> We come to you Father of our Lord Jesus
> We bow to you Father of our Lord Jesus
> We praise you Son of Mary, and yet Son of God
> We call our Hallelujahs to you Jesus Son of our God
> We await your presence in our hearts Spirit eternal.
> We offer you our hearts to be your home O Spirit
>   everlasting.

Trinity praying permeated Celtic lives day and night. Long ago at Clonmacnois, Ireland, Christians prayed beneath huge, hand-sculpted crosses that they called "high crosses." These tall, imposing sculptures were fashioned with geometric art that spoke of the foreverness of God. Here, at these crosses, they often prayed alone to the three-personed God who, because of his inner intimacy at communion, never left them alone. Their own spiritual loneliness was satisfied by the "three of my love." Having seen the fullness of God with the eye of their hearts, they entered into communion with the Trinity and spoke to him out of the longing of their hearts.

What is the lesson for us? Just this: it is not enough to pray in the name of the Trinity, we must become comfortable spending time in communion with the Trinity. For in talking to God in his completeness, we become complete. It is fearsome work to face God's throne and dare to strike up a conversation, but that's what all great living is about!

THE ROLE OF LITANY PRAYER

Once we step up to the final plateau before the throne, the air grows thin, our breath gets short and we "see" God as he truly is. We are shushed by his transcendence. We have too little breath to call his glorious name, for our speaking is checked by his immediacy.

But there is a road through this paralytic awe. Litany praying is to prayer what embassy English is to protocol. Litany praying is a form of response praying led by a worship leader and responded to in more formulaic ways by a gathering of souls. There is something about the Godhead that demands we move away from the colloquial and into the formal. Litany was developed in worship as a way to properly keep our place as we approach his throne. Litany prayer is one path by which the Celts traveled into the Presence.

The Celts were a poetic people, especially at prayer. Simple prose was neither good enough nor ornate enough to address the power at the center of their lives. Poetry was the medium of their deepening love affair with God. As humans cherish God more, they abandon common language in favor of more ornate phrases of praise. The God of the Celts was too personal and too

exalted to be praised with unmeasured words that fell too spontaneously from the tongue. God must be sung to with carefully
formed words that are rehearsed. One must not jabber in the
presence of royalty.

The secular mind sometimes tries to fashion prayers and
generally ends up with a divine headache. But the heart in love
with God cheerfully labors over gladsome poetry. The heart is
the place of prayer rehearsal. It is the editing room for dialogue
with royalty. As long as it works, any old term is generally good
enough for the mind. Not so with the heart. Here the springs of
passion burn hot—hot enough to be a kind of refiner's fire. It is
a foundry of intensity that smelts the ore of our devotion till it
is fine enough to be formed into the highest kind of praise.
Then, and only then, is the word beautiful enough to be spoken. Consider this prayer taken from the *Black Book of Carmarthen*.

> I praise the threefold
> Trinity as God.
> Who is one in three,
> A single power in unity
> His attributes a single mystery,
> One God to praise
> Great King I praise you,
> Great your glory.
> Your Praise is true;
> I am the one who praises you.

This praise, though exalted, is not a litany, yet might easily
pass for one with the simple repetition of any one of its poetic
phrases. But the key is not so much its form but that its source

is the heart. Consider not its rhyming, which is a translator's editing, consider its love and warmth and high praise. Great litanies define our passions, not our creativity. Is it possible that Protestants can deepen their relationship to God merely by litany prayer? I believe they can, but this notion undoubtedly will seem odd to some, particularly to evangelicals. We like spontaneous prayers. But not much poetry is generated spontaneously. Our chatty prayer life may touch reality, but it contains nothing much of high praise. Thus we live much of our lives praying colloquially, "here's how it is, God."

Ian Bradley says that those who are trying to eke out some catalog of Celtic liturgical worship—an entire service of prayer and praise—ultimately will be disappointed, for there is no record of liturgical services during the first two hundred years of Celtic Christianity. We don't know what kind of worship actually went on in those primitive monastic communities. Whether they worshiped out of doors (most likely) or within their primitive, dark, nearly windowless churches (not likely) we don't know. But if the art on their great high crosses is any indication of how they worshiped, it was surely artistic and included abundant storytelling and many group prayers recited from memory. Their love of the Trinity became litanized thus:

> Thou art the pure love of the clouds,
> Thou art the pure love of the skies.
> Thou art the pure love of the stars,
> Thou art the pure love of the moon,
> Thou art the pure love of the sun,
> Thou art the pure love of the heavens,

> Thou art the pure love of the angels,
> Thou art the pure love of Christ himself,
> Thou art the pure love of the God of all life.

Although only the Father and Son are mentioned in this litany, every time the words "pure love" appears, the worshiper is doubtless praying to the entire Trinity.

THE CENTER OF TRINITY PRAYING

Among ancient Celts (of the Irish-Scottish variety), the cultural pre-Christian heroes were the few Celtic elites who could read and write. These literates were not just the local wise men with gifts in poetry and story, they were also writers and thinkers. They were the cultural summation of what the uneducated and uninformed Celts longed to be. They were the Celtic heroes. So much so that Columba is reported to have stated they were his heroes. Yet all who know Columba know that no one was more worthy of his adoration that Jesus Christ. Such simple adoration of Jesus is what we should crave in our lives.

Jesus stands at the center of the Christian faith. And perhaps the real question that comes to us is this: are we willing to accord him the kind of supremacy that Columba readily accorded him? If we answer strongly and in the affirmative—Christ, God in the flesh, stands at the center—then we have to ask ourselves whether we can speak to him with the almighty reverence that the Celtic worshipers did? We must be careful not to answer the question too quickly. For in recent years much of our worship, as exemplified in megachurch "entertainment evangelism," has become so "lite" that Jesus is trivialized as a congenial host who smiles a lot.

The Celtic Christ on the other hand is a Christ who actually dies for our sin, which is as real as he is. We sinners are *mea-culpa* people who need his forgiveness; without it we face perdition. As Patrick himself put it: "the Lord opened the understanding of my unbelieving heart, so that I should relate my sins, even though it was late, and that I should turn with all my heart to the Lord my God" (*Confessions* 2). Among some Protestants, there seems to be a new Christ who is less demanding, and who seems to exist only to coddle the doubtful and to make sure that believers get all the goodies they seek from their secular lives.

Christians need a new view of what the cross is all about. One prominent megachurch pastor told a CBS newsman that his church was doing all it could to appeal to people with no understanding of religion. When the newsman said, "I notice that you have no cross displayed anywhere in your building," The pastor replied, "That's because the cross is offensive to many people." The newsman seemed appreciative of the cleric's common sense. But the Celts would have been less impressed. As one of their modern poets wrote:

The tempests howl, the storms dismay
But manly strength can win the day.
Heave lads, and let the echo ring.

For clouds and squalls will soon pass on,
And victory lie with work well done.
Heave lads, and let the echo ring.

Hold fast! Survive! And all is well,
God sent you worse, He'll calm this swell.

Heave lads, and let the echo ring.

So Satan acts to tire the brain,
And by temptations souls are slain.
Think, lads, of Christ and echo him.

The King of virtues vowed a prize,
For him who wins, for him who tries.
Think, lads, of Christ and echo him.

Trinity praying requires a real Christ for a real day to make real disciples. Any lesser devotion will include only a *little Jesus* who can at best only produce *Christianettes*.

MAKING OUR REQUESTS KNOWN TO THE FULL GODHEAD

As we supplicate the triune God—Father, Son and Holy Spirit—we treasure the glory of their separate offices and yet remember that to seek anything from one is to invoke the response of all. Nonetheless, we find ourselves automatically addressing the separate persons of the Trinity as we seek a specific reply. As I said earlier, it is natural to ask Jesus to meet our day-to-day physical needs, but of course, we also talk to the Son in matters of supplying grace while we seek the comforting presence and empowerment of the Spirit.

At the beginning of the Lord's Prayer stands this plea: "Our Father, . . . give us this day our daily bread." The Bible maintains the notion throughout that the Father is in charge of getting us the bread. It also teaches that God the Father uses the earth's resources to meet all his children needs.

While the Celts asked God to use the weather to bless them

with fish and bread, they didn't often pray for him to end a drought, because rain was common in the British Isles. But on the contrary, in middle America, where I grew up, there were seasons of drought, and at such times we called on the Father to bring rain. When the harvest was abundant, and our thanksgiving was celebrated aloud, just as it had been done centuries before by the Pilgrims:

All is safely gathered in,
Ere the winter storms begin.
God our maker doth provide
For our wants to be supplied.

The Celts thought of God the Father as the supplier, but they did not stop there. They also praised the Son and Spirit for supplying their need. Jesus said, "I and the Father are one" (John 10:30) and "anyone who has seen me has seen the Father" (John 14:9). And we have "access to the Father by one Spirit" (Ephesians 2:18), and the Spirit "searches . . . the deep things of God" (1 Corinthians 2:10). Just as the Father is fully God, so are the Son and the Spirit. There are no levels of subservience within the Trinity. Along with the Father, we too need to see the redeeming Son as supplying our bread and the Holy Spirit as supplying the rain. Father, Son and Spirit are fully involved in both our creation and daily sustenance.

Only Jesus, the Son of God, was incarnated as a human. To him we offer our thanks for his redemption through grace. Neither the Spirit nor the Father bears nail prints in his hands—only the Son does! So we bless him for his sacrifice, and to him we make daily supplication for our sins.

When we need grace in our human frailty, we go especially

to him. When we feel pain, his scars bring us into the fellow-ship of his suffering (Philippians 3:10). Our sacrifice is defined by his (Galatians 2:20). In the extremity of our pain it's difficult to relate to the Holy Spirit and the Father. But pain, it would seem, was the bailiwick of the Son. He is our brother who tasted death (Hebrews 2:9-13). And he is able to bear both our wounds and his. His scars enable him to relate to and care about our suffering. Yet in a mystical sense, redemption, like creation, belongs to all the Godhead at once.

It's difficult for us to imagine the unincarnated Spirit or Father relating to our pain in the same way. Yet we are willing to grant that even Mary suffered as she watched her son die. So can't we by extension believe that the Father suffered when his Son suffered on the cross? Isn't it possible that the Father bore even greater pain when his Son died? Of course it is. And we are sanctified and justified by Jesus Christ and the Spirit (1 Corinthians 6:11). Father, Son and Spirit are all one and fully involved in our redemption.

We supplicate the Spirit for his comforting presence, for the truth, for his fruit in our lives and for our sanctification. He helps us in our weakness by assuring us that we are the children of God, and by praying for us when we don't know how to pray (Romans 8:15-16, 26-27). All of us, ancient Celt or modern Christian, enjoy the abiding presence and ministry of the Spirit.

Being raised in the Pentecostal church, I was used to experiencing God in the person of the Holy Spirit. But the ecstatic joy we feel in the Spirit's personal ministry to us must be understood equally as the visitation of the full Godhead. The Holy Spirit is the Spirit of God (1 Corinthians 3:16) and the Spirit of Jesus Christ (Philippians 1:19). He brings us the presence of both the Father and the Son (John 14:16-18, 26). Father, Son and Spirit are fully involved in our sanctification.

The Celts can teach us to live in the presence of the great Three-in-One through their Trinity prayers. To have the Trinity— our Creator, Redeemer and Sanctifier—at the center of our heart is to experience the full and abundant Christian life. Then we shall stand among the swirling galaxies and cry for joy the benediction found in the *Black Book of Carmathen:*

> I praise the threefold
> Trinity as God
> Who is one in three,
> A single power in unity.

THE PRACTICE OF TRINITY PRAYING

Write your own opening prayer for your regular morning prayer times. Below is a suggestion as to how the prayer might be constructed.

> Gracious Triune Father, Holy Three in One:
>
> I give myself to you in the obedience that is required for the fullest living of this day.
>
> To you Holy Father, I promise to pay attention to:
> the world around me so that I may praise you.
> for all things bright and beautiful.
> for all things wise and wonderful.
> for all creatures great and small.
>
> To you Holy Son, I promise to think about your:
> long-ago life in this world
> and the cost that was required to become like me.

May I prepare to be one with you,
when I have passed the bonds of death
to live more fully in your presence.

To you Holy Spirit, I promise to treasure your:
moment-by-moment abiding in my life.
I promise that I will not be casual in my regard for
your inner presence.
I want to hold you in the altar of my heart
so that I may treasure your never ending presence.

Amen.

Using the example to be completed below, write your own sunrise prayer by completing these sentences.

Holy God,
I am rising today in the name of the Father who

I am rising today in the name of the Son who

I am rising today in the name of the Spirit who

Using the example to be completed below, write your own bedtime prayer by completing these sentences.

God of all that is and was and shall be,
for this day and its fullness I give you thanks;

Thank you Father for the Earth and for its endless beauty.
Thank you especially for

Thank you, Son, for, your example of obedience
to your Father which taught me faithfulness this day
as I endeavored to

Thank you, Spirit, for your infilling of my life,
I especially thank you for your presence to day
as you walked with me through

Father, give me sleep tonight, so that my praise in the morning may

Son, wake me in obedience tomorrow so that I may

Spirit, offer me your presence tomorrow so that I may

Amen.

The Scriptures stood on the edge of this fragile material world

and offered a vision of a more lasting world.

THOMAS O'LOUGHLIN

The world was now,
for the Christian,
just hovering on the edge of being.
The call for the Christian was to move
To its very limit and peer beyond.
This could take place in reflection
While walking and working,
or in decoding the Scriptures,
and in the liturgy
Christians could actually
Experience praising God with
the inhabitants of that higher world:
the angels and powers,
and cherubim and seraphim,
the choir of the apostles and prophets,
and the white robed army of the martyrs.
Whether walking, working,
reading or praying,
one was in two worlds:
this physical world which seemed to be real,
but which was fragile and slipping away,
moment by moment,
and the spiritual world,
which was intangible, clouded the senses,
but which was real.

THOMAS O'LOUGHLIN

2

SCRIPTURE PRAYER

Praying the Bible Back to Its Author

At Clonmacnois, Ireland, I once stood dwarfed beneath a great stone cross, emblazoned fifteen hundred years earlier with the Gospels in picture. Why had the sculptor carved these images from the Gospels? Because artists carve or write or sing what is most important to them. The Celts, like all other lovers of God, wanted to give back to God all that was most significant in their lives.

Even more impressive than the high cross of Clonmacnois is the Book of Kells, now housed at Trinity College in Dublin. The manuscript is thirteen hundred years old and was produced by a group of monks working on vellum with ink and paint to produce an artistic volume that would give back to God as he had given to them.

Still Celts—like so many primitive cultures—believed that the most powerful word was the spoken word. The spoken word was free; it flew on oral wings. But the written word was frozen to the page, and its stoic and literary heart forbade it to live. Writing robbed communication of its mobility and power. To these ancient God-lovers, spoken words were the more spontaneous stuff of praise and love.

As a husband of forty-seven years, I realize that the most holistic—the most worthwhile—gift I can give my wife is what she has always given me: love! All other gifts I can buy are but trinkets. The love that fuels her life is what I long to give back to her, and I must speak it aloud for it to really count. The Celts sweltered under the heat of divine love. What greater gift could they celebrate than what had been so significant to them? If the Gospels were God's Word to them, their gift to him was giving it back.

On the other side of the centuries, I have often found myself praying the ancient prayers of the *Carmina Gadelica*. What is the *Carmina Gadelica*? It is a collection of Celtic songs and prayers gathered into a large, single volume of adoration and praise, entreaty and thanksgiving. It is a millennial echo of those ancient brothers and sisters of ours whose devotion ever challenges us toward our own discovery of the inner life of Christ. But why would anyone want to study this folksy anthem of devotion? Because we can think of nothing better to offer God than the words of glory first offered by those whose lives were both hard and temporary. Their most meaningful gifts to God were their prayers!

PRAYING GOD'S WORD BACK TO HIM

I recently stayed for a week at Glenstall Abbey near Limerick, Ireland. I went to matins, lauds, vespers and complines every day. Over and over I heard a group of sixty monks giving the Psalms and Gospels back to God in the mesmerizing beauty of

Gregorian chants. They were Benedictines, not Celts, but their offerings to God—five times a day—was the Word of God. These men live simply. They own nothing and may not receive a gift, any gift, without the abbot's permission. But their lives are devoted to Scripture, which they read—and pray—back to God during an astounding thirty-five worship services per week. That's 1,820 worship services a year!

Further, they have committed themselves to silence during the evening meal—and this silence continues through the 6:30 a.m. service every morning. Though they are silent, they often listen to Mozart or a reading from the lives of saints. They learn to listen to God often and for long periods of time, and when they're not listening to God, they're often talking to God by praying his Word back to him. In praying God's Word back to him, the Bible becomes a vast book of praise. This is why *lectio divina* has become so popular throughout the ages. The *lectio divina* is the reading of God's Word without commentary or added human sentiment. The actual practice of *lectio divina* is not Celtic in its origins. Still the Celts believed in the concept that spoken Scripture—unadorned by commentary was the heart of faith. They seemed to believe there was a deliberate power for living in and allowing the Bible to have its own majestic voice without the clutter of human chitchat trying to explain it.

Some Scriptures are easier to pray than others. Many passages in Leviticus, for example, would be difficult to offer as a prayer. The Psalms, on the other hand, are the poetry of adoration. Little wonder that Celtic psalters arose early as the soul of prayer and praise.

But the issue isn't so much which kind of passages are easier to pray but our view of Scripture itself. If we merely see Scripture as God's Word that we need to apply, we will certainly find *some* vitality in praying. But this may not be the optimum way to view Scripture. We would do well to see it as the Celts did. They saw Scripture—according to Thomas O'Loughlin, a contemporary Celtic scholar—as literature born on the high ledges between this world and the next.

O'Loughlin sees the Celtic view of Scripture as paralleling a view set forth by Eucherius, bishop of Lyons and a contemporary of Augustine. Eucherius, much like the writer of Revelation, noted that all sorts of things in the Bible, natural and human, were related by an invisible but decipherable code. For example, Eucherius wrote:

> So, for instance when we meet the word field (*ager*) in scripture (it occurs 253 times in the Latin Bible) what does it mean? Christ (what better interpreter could there be?) tells us it signifies this world of ours (Mt. 13:38). So whenever we meet "field" (upon the authority of scripture itself) we can read this word as a code word pointing to a higher realm where (for those who know the code) it means world.

This form of Scripture interpretation definitely would not appeal to modern critical scholars. But for the credulous of Eucherius's time (who saw the Bible as a book of mysterious codes) it was dynamite.

Is this a contradiction between the Celts treasuring simple Bible reading (remember, illiteracy was high among the Celts so they often memorized what they couldn't read) and the kind of formal study required to see Scripture as needing commentary and explanation? Not at all. The monks and scholars among them always studied and determined to know as much as they might about Scripture—as have scholars in every culture. Still scholars knew that the simple reading of the Bible uninterrupted by critical thinking or warm insights was a powerful mode of worship.

Eucherius seemed to prove that

the Scriptures stood on the edge of a mysterious fragile world and offered a vision of a more lasting world.

Since the Scriptures used images from this world, yet told of heaven, the very things in the word could, for those with the eyes of faith, be symbols of a higher world. . . . This world was now, for the Christian, just hovering at the edge of being. The call to the Christian was to move to its very limit and peer beyond. This could take place in reflection while walking and working, or in decoding the Scriptures, and in the liturgy, Christians could actually experience praising God with the inhabitants of that higher world: the angels and powers, the cherubim and seraphim, the choir of the apostles and prophets, and the white-robed army of martyrs. . . . Christian life was in many senses a journey along the edge.

It's easy to see why the Bible, with its powerful inner mysteries, became the center of Celtic devotion. To merely repeat its words aloud was to draw forth power. Because of our wealth, our self-centered, materialistic, consumer culture, and our adoption of a rationalistic worldview, we perceive little of the edgy living on display in God's book. We would be far more likely to pray the Scriptures if we saw it as the Celts did: an edgy book not to be treated lightly.

A key to praying the Scriptures is making it more personal. For example, "The LORD is my shepherd" becomes, "Lord, *you* are my shepherd. . . . *You* make me to lie down in green pastures. . . . *You* restore my soul. *You* lead me in paths of righteousness." And the Magnificat becomes, "My soul glorifies you, O Lord."

In helping us to pray the Scriptures as the Celts would have, I will address five approaches that are presented in the various chapters of this book.

TRINITY PRAYER

Consider Trinity praying. When the poet John Donne wrote "batter my heart, three personed God," he was addressing the particular God of history who identified himself as the God of Abraham, Isaac and Jacob, and "wrestled" with all three in Canaan. He is the one who brought the Hebrews into Canaan and formed them into a nation. He is the one who called Mary "blessed." He is Father of the eternal Son—Jesus Christ. He is a well-defined and very personal God.

In praying the Scriptures holistically, the Trinity must be kept in mind. Though the word *Trinity* isn't used in the Bible, the Scriptures are Trinity saturated. For example, the world came to be when God created the heavens and earth. But the Scripture also says the Spirit of God hovered over this early creation (Genesis 1:2). And even though the Son of God doesn't make his glorious appearance until the Gospels, the apostle Paul informs us that the Son, too, was involved in creation (Colossians 1:16).

To pray in a trinitarian fashion is to take a biblical metaphor that describes some characteristic of the Father or Christ or the Spirit and enlarge it by applying it to the other two Persons. Often in Celtic trinitarian statements, for instance, the Father is denoted as King, Christ as Lord and the the third Person is designated the Holy Spirit. Thus we might pray, "The King is my shepherd; the Lord is my shepherd; the Spirit is my shepherd." And it doesn't take a great leap to read Psalm 46 as "God is my refuge and strength; Christ is my refuge and strength; the Spirit is my refuge and strength." We don't need to do this every time we run into a divine name, but remembering to do it every once in a while fixes at our soul's center how we see the Trinity in relationship to ourselves. It is *never* appropriate, of course, to alter the Bible to fit our own schemes. We need to be careful about confusing the important biblical and doctrinal distinctions of the Father, the Son and the Holy Spirit. But we ought to use the Bible in our private prayers to remind ourselves of the fullness of the Godhead.

LISTENING PRAYER

Why is praying Scripture so important? First, it's the best way to develop the art of listening prayer. We too often go into God's presence with a list of pleas, trying to talk God into granting our desires. But this kind of praying makes us "one big mouth" and God "one grand ear." But when we pray the Scriptures, it makes God the voice and leaves us as the ear. In short, God gets his turn at getting a word in edgewise.

Second, listening prayer reminds us that prayer is not merely about us. It's the path to true union with the Trinity. Reading the author's Word back to him binds us into union with him.

Once at a poetry reading I was reciting one of my poems for children to a very large crowd. I looked down to see a very small boy whose lips were moving in sync with mine. The sight of it stopped me.

"Son," I said, startling the boy, "do you know this poem by heart?"

In an exaggerated manner, he shook his head affirmatively.

"Could you come up here and do it for us all?" I asked.

He bolted away from his parents and ran up on the stage. I handed him the mic and he recited the poem to me—the author. For one brief, shining moment he and I were one—author and reader.

This same oneness lies at the heart of all classic works on prayer. Many Christians have been steeped in the prayer of Jabez, recited mostly in hope that God would "enlarge their territory" (1 Chronicles 4:10). In contemporary terms, this generally means, "Lord, won't you give me a Mercedes-Benz." But the best of saints have seldom prayed to get stuff from God. Instead, they are after union with Christ. They want to live in the center of all that God is, with the twofold purpose of serving him and enjoying him forever. That's the intent God has for our prayers.

Seeing ourselves (rather than God) as the ear leaves God free to speak to us and to call us into the center of himself. Then we may say with Paul: "My goal is to know him and the power of his resurrection and the fellowship of his sufferings, being conformed to his death" (Philippians 3:10, my translation).

Does our listening prayer need to be done in silence only, or can it be prayed orally? Both. At least some of the time our prayers ought to be said aloud. When we pray Scripture aloud, it provides an empirical reinforcement that a silent reading doesn't offer. To pray the Scriptures aloud strengthens our prayers in two ways. First, it focuses our attention. When we pray silently, our prayers are apt to be interrupted by those pesky thoughts that bounce around inside our heads. But once we give our prayers volume, they gain a stronger life and focus. Thus we are more likely to find a detour-free road to God.

There is another principle I learned about prayer through editing my books. I always make my final edit by reading a book aloud (preferably to an accompanying editor). I have discovered that during this reading, I can hear what's good or bad about my writing. Something magical occurs when I force my silent words out into the open and let them reenter my mind through the air and eardrum. This has taught me that a silent prayer usually doesn't give as much attention to the form it takes as a spoken prayer does. And when addressing the triune God, careful attention ought to be made. Praying the Scriptures with a listening ear allows us to really hear ourselves as we address God, which is not a casual, come-what-may affair.

Third, we want to pray God's Word to him that it may make us one with him and also unite us to his body, the church. When coupled with *lectio divina*, listening prayer is a group activity that enhances corporate prayer and worship.

Corporate praying the Scriptures is unitive. There are few things more important than the unity of the body of Christ. I remember when the astronauts read from the book of Genesis on their moon voyage. What a sense of unity we sensed when we were fused into common humanity. Though separated by a great distance, the astronauts and the earthbound were made one when the astronaut read God's Word. This same sense of oneness is ours when as a body we pray Scripture to God. Nothing is more beautiful than a church praying the Lord's Prayer. Why? Partly because we—the many—become one when we pray the Scripture back to God.

LONG, WANDERING PRAYER

The peregrini, traveling Celts, were on a lifelong, shrineless pilgrimage; their only altar lay in eternity. Their pilgrimage was a listening journey. As they read the Bible, they entered into God's presence and heard from him as they sojourned. Likewise, praying Scripture is our conversation with God in the ongoing pilgrimage of life.

We can see this notion of life as a pilgrimage in many of our hymns. For example,

> I'm pressing on the upward way,
> New heights I'm gaining every day;
> Still praying as I onward bound,
> Lord, plant my feet on higher ground.

Or

> O Beulah Land, sweet Beulah Land,
> As on the highest mount I stand,
> I look away across the sea,
> Where mansions are prepared for me,
> And see the heavenly, glory shore,
> My Heav'n, my home forever more.

Scriptures of praise can be the ongoing anthems of our pilgrimage. How gloriously might we pray the Psalms of Ascent or the Revelation passages of the apostle John or the "third heaven" passage of Paul from 2 Corinthians.

But the Celts did not solely use the praise passages in their prayers to God. They also included Scriptures that speak of Christ's ability to overcome our trials. We too can pray the Scriptures of trial in which God instructs the pitiful, life-trampled Job to listen to the almighty nature of the overcoming God. Then too there is John 14, where Jesus counsels, "Do not let your hearts be troubled." Or we might pray from the epistle of James, where he counsels us to remember that our many trials will make us "mature and complete."

The Celts felt God's omnipotence when they recited the *Biáit* (Psalm 119). There is a story of the abbot of Cill Becain that demonstrates how the Celts saw the power of quoted Scripture.

Maol Póil Ó Cinnaetha, abbot of the monastery of Cill Becain, had been discussing astrology with another monk. After that, in his sleep, he saw this Gospel Nun who had died six days previously coming towards him complaining bitterly that it didn't matter to him that she was dead. "How are things with you there, O Woman?" said he. "Little you care, indeed," said she, "discussing astrology without making intercession for me. . . . Miserable your performance," said she. "What form of intercession do you require from me, O Woman?' said he. "The *Biáit,* of course," said she, "the *Biáit* after the *Biáit,* the *Biáit* above the *Biáit,* the *Biáit* below the *Biáit,*" said she, all in one breath, ordering that the *Biáit* should be said often for her, for nothing except the Mass for the Dead alone is held in greater esteem by God than the *Biáit*.

There is a great spiritual power made available to us in our trials simply from quoting the Scripture.

When I am defeated by my failures to overcome sin, I pray Romans 7:25—8:1: "I thank God through Jesus Christ our Lord! So then, with my mind I myself am a slave to the law of God, but with my flesh, to the law of sin. Therefore, no condemnation now exists for those in Christ Jesus" (HCSB). When I pass through the valley of the shadows, I read Psalm 23 as a prayer to God. When my pilgrimage brings me grief, I pray 1 Corinthians 15:51-58. I recommend 2 Timothy 4 as a great passage for a person to pray when he or she is getting ready to pass life's final gates.

The Benedictines usually begin and end the various segments of their Gregorian chants with antiphons, which are sung responsively. When marking out the great pilgrimage passages of the Bible, it might be good to develop some antiphon passages to begin and close our Scripture prayer. There are several that convince me I can be a better steward of my brief sojourn on earth. I treasure these verses, repeating them daily between my Scripture prayers.

> Teach us to number our days carefully
> so that we may develop wisdom in our hearts.
> (Psalm 90:12 HCSB)

For I am already being poured out as a drink offering, and the time for my departure is close. I have fought a good fight, I have finished the race, I have kept the faith. In the future, there is reserved for me the crown of righteousness, which the Lord, the righteous Judge, will give me on that day, and not only to me, but to all those who have loved His appearing. (2 Timothy 4:6-8 HCSB)

I also like Psalm 37:3 and Isaiah 55:1:

Trust in the Lord and do what is good;
   dwell in the land and live securely. (Psalm 37:3 HCSB)

Come, everyone who is thirsty,
   come to the waters; and you without money,
   come, buy, and eat!
   Come, buy wine and milk
   without money and without cost! (Isaiah 55:1 HCSB)

Because I have memorized these "antiphon" texts, it's easy to include them at the conclusion of any Scripture I pray. And I never cease to pray, for the pilgrimage is long and my need is great.

NATURE PRAYER

It is a wonderful thing to take your Bible outdoors to spend time in praise. There are great passages from Genesis that need to be prayed outside. The last five chapters of the book of Job are splendid Scriptures to pray outdoors. So are almost any of the psalms that focus on nature—Psalm 19 or 23 or 46 or 90. The mountains are a great place to read Isaiah 40. Harvest is a wonderful time to read John 4. Of course, the birth narratives of Matthew and Luke should be read at Christmas. Epiphany is the occasion to pray Matthew 28 or Luke 1. All out of doors! The seashore is a fine place to pray from the book of Jonah or any of the Galilean passages, beginning with Matthew 4.

One of my most enjoyable times of Scripture prayer was when I prayed, in New Zealand, the "Great Shepherd" and "I Am" texts of John. The sheep are so abundant in that beautiful land that it's impossible to not think of John 10. How easy and meaningful it was to pray these passages in the midst of God's great creation.

It's important to mind the time of day certain Scriptures are read. Evening is a great time to read the Passion narratives. Pray through the resurrection story in the early morning. Mid-morning is a splendid time to pray the Sermon on the Mount. Romans 8 or Philippians 2 will speak loudly when you are preparing to retire for the day.

Outdoor nature praying is a splendid way to pray the Scriptures. As you do, let the prayers be punctuated with silence. I have found that the silent places are often filled with the very presence of the triune Author of the holy Word.

The key is to read your Bible somewhere outdoors—far beyond the busy confines of the office or home. For example, in a church I pastored we often selected the last week in October as Bible Focus Week. On Wednesday of that week we placed a Bible on the pulpit and assigned four hundred couples to come to the church at all hours of the day. Each read the Bible aloud for a quarter hour, taking over where the last left off.

This may not seem to be nature praying, but those who arrived in the middle of the night said that it was both eerie and exotic. The dark world through which they traveled to get to the church was alive with mystery in the wee hours of morning. So, as they each took their turn at reading the Bible aloud, they confessed to feeling God's presence in very real ways. In some ways the midnight readers felt the same exotic darkness that surrounds the midnight service on Christmas Eve, when the cool air and—in Nebraska, where I pastored—the sometimes falling snow sharpened our Scripture prayers into the most exotic of conversations between creature and Creator.

Prayer is like any other kind of communication. There are times when meaning is shared, but there is no real excitement. At other times, though, the mood is so pregnant with joy it's impossible to forget. We pray God's Word and suddenly God encompasses us with his presence. Our union with the Godhead is like heady wine, intoxicating us with the Scriptures that we imbibe.

Corporate Scripture prayer is enhanced in many natural settings: under a starlit sky, around a crackling fire, on a lakeshore with gently lapping waters, in a canopied forest, watching the sun rise in the cool of the morning. All Scripture reading is treasured. But praying the Scriptures outdoors is special—because God's grandeur is exhibited in and enhanced by nature as we stand in its midst to celebrate him.

LORICA PRAYER

Seeking God's protection in an uncertain world is where the Celts really excelled. They found assurance of his care in the truths of the Bible. So when they prayed their lorica—their breastplate of protection—they were calling on the most certain power they knew to protect them on their journey into a future they didn't know at all. In their lorica they prayed Scripture such as these:

> I love you, LORD, my strength.
> The LORD is my rock, my fortress, and my deliverer,
>   my God, my mountain where I seek refuge,

my shield and the horn of my salvation, my stronghold.
I called to the Lord, who is worthy of praise,
    and I was saved from my enemies.
The ropes of death were wrapped around me;
    the torrents of destruction terrified me.
The ropes of Sheol entangled me;
    the snares of death confronted me.
I called to the LORD in my distress,
    and I cried to my God for help.
    From His temple He heard my voice,
    and my cry to Him reached His ears. (Psalm 18:1-6 HCSB)

Every passage of Scripture is such a powerful word from God that just its reading lifts the despairing to new vistas of hope.

In all my years as a pastor, I counted it a great joy to read the Scriptures to those who were ill. There is something healing in the mere opening of the Word of God. Every part of the Word is a lorica of protection. All of it heals. All of it confidently readies the bearer for what lies ahead. If I had my ministry to live through all over again, I would read the Bible even more often than I did the first time—acknowledging freely that the Word of God merely spoken has intrinsic power to heal and protect. This is not to see it as some amulet of magic but rather to let it be what is has been for saints in every era—God continuing to speak his healing word to human need.

LET THE WORD TRANSPORT YOU

The key in all of our Scripture praying is to let the Word become the mode of our transport. Scripture is not just the basis or background of our praying but a prayer itself. When we are reading the Scripture, the border between Scripture and prayer become so thin that they meld into each other and we are united with God. At such times our separation is bridged, and we are transported into the very presence of the holy Trinity.

Praying the Scriptures can become a way to make all areas of prayer effective. It can be used to add substance to each of the other models of prayer, providing the context that makes all forms beautiful and effective.

When I was a boy, the first telephone I had ever seen was in my married sister's home. To get the operator, the caller had to hold down on the receiver hook and turn a crank that tripped a magneto, causing the bells to wring on other phones (it was what was known as a "party line"). Suddenly some voice would appear at the other end. (Actually, there were usually ten other busybodies who picked up their phones just to listen in.) As quaint as this may seem now, I was amazed that it could be done and I thrilled at this new rural technology that allowed people to speak over long distances. Likewise, when I learned to pray the Scriptures, I was amazed that the distance between myself and the triune God was reduced to an immediate oneness.

In country churches we had a song that likened prayer to these rustic telephones. The lyrics counseled, "Central's never busy, always on the line, / You may hear from heaven almost anytime." Scripture prayer is the most forceful kind of communication with God I have discovered. God is waiting to hear his words spoken back to him through your life.

THE PRACTICE OF SCRIPTURE PRAYING

One way to incorporate Scripture praying into your spiritual life is to create your own midday Scripture prayer. Here's an example of how we might pray Scripture.

God,

I come to you, made more alive by your own Word revealed in holy Scripture.

I offer you this prayer:

In the beginning was the Word, and the Word was with God, and the Word was God. He was with God in the beginning.

Through him all things were made; without him nothing was made that has been made. In him was life, and that life was the light of men. The light shines in the darkness, but the darkness has not understood it. . . .

Yet to all who received him, to those who believed in his name, he gave the right to become children of God—children born not of natural descent, nor of human decision or a husband's will, but born of God. (John 1:1-5, 12-13 NIV)

In the name of the Father and of the Son and of the Holy Ghost,

Amen.

In the next prayer, consider the passage you have just prayed with some personalizing reflections. Below is a suggestion as to how the prayer might be constructed.

God,

I come to you, made more alive with your own words. I offer you this prayer:

In the beginning was the Word, and the Word was with God, and the Word was God.

Whenever the beginning was I know I existed already in your heart, O Christ. Even then, was I loved by the Word of God who waited only till the fullness of time had come to show me his love.

He was with God in the beginning.

Through him all things were made; without him nothing was made that has been made.

I was made. I have a Maker. I stand in the middle of creation and exult that he who made the world made me as well and that on the sixth day. He exulted, "It is good!" The heavens declare your glory O God, the earth shows your handiwork. I was made for you, and by you, for reasons of your own.

In him was life, and that life was the light of men.

As you are light, may I walk in you. Teach me to avoid darkness so that all my thoughts and deeds are shadowless deeds—no darkness at all—which I gladly offer back to you.

The light shines in the darkness, but the darkness has not understood it. . . .

Yet to all who received him, to those who believed in his name, he gave the right to become children of God—children born not of natural descent, nor of human decision or a husband's will, but born of God. (John 1:1-5, 12-13)

I believe in the name. I receive the one whose name is Wonderful, Counselor, the mighty God, the Prince of Peace. Thank you that my birthright is in heaven. For I have been born not of natural descent, nor through any act of human will, but I have been born again, of the water and the Spirit. I have a new name. It is Christian. I have been named after him who was unbegotten and eternal.
Amen.

Studying the prayer above, write your own interpolations:

God, I come to you made more alive with your own words. I offer you this prayer:

In the beginning was the Word, and the Word was with God, and the Word was God.

He was with God in the beginning. Through him all things were made; without him nothing was made that has been made.

In him was life, and that life was the light of men.

The light shines in the darkness, but the darkness has not understood it. . . . Yet to all who received him, to those who believed in his name, he gave the right to become children of God—children born not of natural descent, nor of human decision or a husband's will, but born of God (John 1:1-5, 12-13).

Amen.

Pilgrimage is ultimately about hope.

Pilgrims are above all else seekers.

Ian Bradley,
Celtic Christian Communities

3

LONG, WANDERING PRAYER

Seeing Life as a Single, Unending Prayer

Everyday you depart, everyday you return," preached Columbanus. It was not in Celtic literature that I first discovered this truth, nor in Ireland but in Birmingham, Alabama. Each morning, somewhere around six, I drive thirty-two miles to work. Each afternoon, around four, I return. During these moments at the wheel, in the hustle and bustle of heavy traffic, I have encountered the fatigue of the journey. I am locked bumper to bumper with thousands of fellow travelers who are far too prone to annoy me rather than bless me with their company.

It's the road that defines my day, and yet it isn't. I know where the road is going, but I have lost all interest in the scenery. I know if I could meet some of my fellow travelers around a campfire, we would likely become good friends. But I am shut up in that modern monastic cell called the automobile. And there I listen to Christian music. And there I pray, with eyes straight ahead, for all that makes a multitasking disciple grow quiet and whole in a buzzing, honking, rubber-on-concrete world.

I am en route, that is all. But not quite all. I want to know Christ better, and in order to get to know him better I must do it while I am en route. I am a twenty-first-century "goer" in search of a settled sabbath. I have been ordained a pilgrim by the never-ending, roaring concrete, and I am what the Celts would have called a peregrine. I must practice the presence of God where God seems seems to be absent. In this modern matrix, I have found a sixth-century hero named Brendan, whose exploits at spiritual pilgrimage were not recorded till the tenth century. Brendan's life was that of a *peregrinatio pro Christi,* a wanderer for Christ. And his wanderings are no more spectacular than his faith. He prayed as he sailed his small crafts through the Hebrides. He was not out to map this uncharted world. His reasons for sailing lay elsewhere.

Brendan was the great navigator of the Celts, but his real voyage was to find union with Christ. Apparently, he was lured to this fantastic voyage to the "promised land of the saints" by Barinthus, a monastery colleague and grandson of the king, who had reportedly been to that land. That land, said Barinthus, was full of flowers and precious stones. Brendan felt impelled to find it so he could become acquainted with the men and women of God who lived in that resplendent isle of holiness. Thus he had his coracle (a boat) fitted with sail and rudder, and set out with fellow pilgrims to find this delicious (and near delirious) land. When the wind died and the sail hung limp, the men rowed, though they knew not where. Finally Brendan ordered the fatigued rowers to stop. He cried, "God is our helper. He is our navigator and helmsman, and he shall guide us. Pull in the oars and the rudder. Spread the sail and let God do as he wishes with his servants and their boat." And God filled the sails.

Brendan reportedly had many spectacular experiences, like setting up camp on the back of the sea monster named Jasconius (which he believed to be an island) and visiting with the shaggy-headed Judas, the betrayer of Christ, who here and there throughout eternity receives a temporary respite from hell. Brendan's tale seems more like a Ulysses adventure than an account of a spiritually hungry pilgrim. Nonetheless, his is the story of a saint who longed to move ever closer to the source of his salvation, Christ.

Brendan wasn't the only seafaring Celtic pilgrim. Some scholars believe a few peregrini might have made it all the way to America because of some otherwise unexplainable Celtic inscriptions found in West Virginia. Whether or not these Celtic sailors beat Leif Erickson and Columbus to North America, it is certain they sailed to Iceland. But these world-travelers weren't like the Spanish conquistadors. They weren't seeking treasures, but the reward of spiritual obedience. Just as God had called Abraham to "Leave your country, your people and your father's household and go to the land I will show you" (Genesis 12:1), they were called to leave Ireland and Scotland for God's purposes. "Let us praise God," says the Black Book of Carmarthen, "at the beginning and the end of time. Whoever seeks him out, He will not deny or refuse." This cry of the heart implies that God is on the side of the seeker. He longs for union with the seeker even more than those who seek him.

ISLAND-HOPPING VERSUS TRAILBLAZING

Brendan's voyages teach us that we are ever journeying to new vistas of our mortality, so God can reveal something more of his nature to us. Brendan's biography is filled with metaphors that expose life not as we see it with spiritually dull eyes but as it really is.

On the island Brendan meets Judas Iscariot, the betrayer of Jesus! Judas explains that, by the mercy of Jesus, he is on the island for a brief respite from his never-ending suffering in hell.

> "I am Judas, most wretched, and the greatest traitor. I am here not on account of my own merits but because of the mysterious mercy of Jesus Christ. For me this is not a place of torment but rather a place of respite granted me by the Savior in honor of his Resurrection." It was the Lord's own day. "It seems to me when I sit here that I am in the Garden of Delights in comparison with the agonies which I know I shall suffer this evening. For I burn like molten lead in a crucible day and night at the heart of the mountain which you see, where Leviathan lives with his companions. I have a respite here every Sunday from first to second vespers, from Christmas until Epiphany, from Easter until Pentecost, and on the Feast of the Purification and the Assumption of the Mother of God. The rest of the year I am tortured in the depths of hell with Herod and Pilate, Annas and Caiaphas. Therefore I beseech you by the Savior of the world to be kind enough to intercede for me with the Lord Jesus Christ that I may be allowed to remain here until sunset tomorrow and that the devils may not torment me, seeing your arrival here, and drag me off to the hideous destiny which I purchased with so terrible a price." St. Brendan replied: "The Lord's will be done. You shall not be consumed by devils tonight until dawn."

Needless to say, this is a fanciful tale, but Judas's experience should warn Christians about the dangers of sin and the grace of God in Christ.

And in his travels, Columba, says his biographer, was the first to encounter the Loch Ness monster. When one of his companions was attacked by Nessie, Columba made the sign of the cross and rebuked Leviathan, saying "Thou shalt go no further, nor touch the man; go back with all speed." What is being celebrated here is the power of the cross over the demonic dragons in all of life. We shouldn't let Nessie's reality, or nonreality, distract us from the real message of the peregrini. They were on a journey of prayer through strange seas and lands. They were praying pilgrims, journeying through trust to serve the living God. Hugh Connolly wrote:

> The Celtic image of pilgrimage affords a vision of the Christian life wherein the individual will inevitably encounter suffering and sin, but where he also has the means, through penance, to cleave to that graced process, whereby he is freed from the un-Christ-like elements which impede the growth of his humanity into the kingdom.

In Brendan's and Columba's travels we learn of heaven and hell, life and death, sin and the gospel, and the triune God. Each adventure becomes a new picture, a new metaphor, a new way to teach us about the nature and power of the Trinity and the gospel of Christ.

Faith is never a resting place. As soon as new disciples enter the fortress of faith, they find they must leave again. They willingly take up the dangerous life of a world-changer. Change has come to them personally along with a command to effect in the world what they have lately experienced. Bringing more change.

Thomas O'Loughlin calls his dynamic book on this subject *Journeys on the Edges*. The call of the peregrini is to do something in this life that has other-worldly consequences. A call to serve Christ means that we have accepted a mystical job description: all of our service must be done in this world for the sake of the next. O'Loughlin spells it out for us:

> Whether walking, working, reading or praying, one is in two worlds; this physical world, which seems so real but which is fragile and slipping away moment by moment, and the spiritual world which is intangible, clouded the senses, but which is real; and if one had not a lasting city here (Heb. 131:14) then it was by no means certain that one had been granted a place in the kingdom. Christian life is in many senses a journey along the edge.

This philosophy makes the Christ followers the happiest people on earth. When the present world is seen through spiritual eyes, true treasures are found where others would never think to look.

Those who confess live on the edge. The edge is where pilgrimages are born. The world becomes a "going" place rather than a residing place. The Bible is a book about and for edge-dwellers. Abraham traveled to a land he had never seen (Genesis 12:1-5). Moses moved from a life of luxury to the deserts (Exodus 2:15). Jesus "had no place to lay his head" (Luke 9:58), and the apostles were sent to the "ends of the earth" (Acts 1:8). Properly seen the peregrini were not doing anything out of the ordinary when they sailed without compass to strange lands. They were being wholly consistent with Scripture.

PRAYING WITHOUT CEASING

We sometimes wonder about Paul's admonition to pray without ceasing (1 Thessalonians 5:17). Can we do it? Is it really possible? One thing is for sure, the key is to see prayer as something we *are* instead of something we *do*. Long, wandering prayer is that sort of defining prayer. It is the lifelong journey between the "Our Father in heaven" and "We ask these things in the name of Christ." The life of pilgrimage praying isn't merely *punctuated* by prayer. The pilgrimage *is* the prayer. The peregrini weren't going somewhere to pray, they were praying as they went, wherever they went. They were pilgrims without a shrine. Life wasn't a destination. Life was the journey. They never really "arrived," so they never stopped praying.

Whatever our apparent earthly destinations, our life itself is a pilgrimage. Once we understand we will never "arrive," we can remain in a continual state of prayer. This doesn't mean we are always talking to God. The fullest definition of long, wandering prayer is journeying in the presence of the triune God. And even when our hearts are not wrapped (or rapt) in conversation with the Almighty, we are yet in his presence.

Whether we talk or listen to God, we are to live in the lifelong abundance of his presence. This sort of presence is the bedrock of long, wandering prayer. This is why my long trek to work and back is fulfilling. God and I are not always in verbal contact, but his presence is real. Thus I am able to define my morning commute as a long, wandering prayer.

What is the basis of our union with God? Why does his presence endure? The answer to both questions is God's Son. As the best of Irish poets and mystics saw it, the cross was a bridge between this world where we dwell temporarily and that higher world where God reigns eternal. God, in his grace, redeemed us through his Son's incarnation, life, death and resurrection. There is a yearning to make peace—to become one—in God's love. And in Christ our yearnings to be united with God are satisfied. Here the yearnings of the great Trinity and the needy pilgrim meet.

EARTHBOUND HELP FOR THE NEEDY PILGRIM

Prayer need not be a solo trip. According to James 5:13-16 the needy should pray with and for each other. Indeed this is why God gave us the church. Brendan did not navigate the seas alone. Likewise, there's room on our journey for soul friends (or prayer partners). When we engage in long, wandering prayer with such friends, we discover a broader dimension of union with Christ. As an ancient Jewish wise man said:

> A faithful friend is a secure shelter;
>> whoever finds one, finds a treasure.
> A faithful friend is beyond price;
>> there is no measure of his worth.
> A faithful friend is an elixir of life,
>> found only by those who fear the Lord.
> (Ecclesiasticus 6:14-16 REB)

The Celtic model is not one of short-term or occasional friendship, but as a daily commitment throughout life. The novelist George Eliot wrote of this kind of friendship: "Oh the comfort, the inexpressible comfort of feeling safe with a person; having neither to weigh thoughts nor measure words, but to pour them all out, just as they are, chaff and grain together, knowing that a faithful hand will take and sift them, keep what is worth keeping, and then, with the breath of kindness, blow the rest away."

Life can be viewed as one long prayer journey. If we follow the example of the peregrini, the implications for our world-view are enormous. Their prayer life and mission work were never finished. In fact, most of these Celtic mariners didn't return home because they saw themselves as perpetual exiles. Sadly, we *do* view this world as our home, and we are captive both to it and our churchy materialistic lifestyles. How can we regain our lost sense of pilgrimage?

THE TEMPORARY SERVICE AND THE
TEMPORARY SHRINE

In Chaucer's *Canterbury Tales* we find a group of pilgrims journeying to the shrine of St. Thomas at Canterbury. Once there, they pass the time by prayers and vigils, but soon their spiritual experience is over, and they all trudge back to their dreary home lives. This, I'm afraid, is how most of us view pilgrimage. The peregrine pilgrimage was different than that of Chaucer's pilgrims.

For these sailors, the horizon was the call. Every island they touched was a place to discover something new about God. We need to view the voyages as metaphorical in nature. Just as Brendan's travel was informed by these wild experiences, so our life journey of long, wandering prayer can be shaped by unimaginable encounters with the three-personed God.

But what kind of Christ would call Brendan into the wilds of the sea, where the waves pounded and the winds blew? What does this Christ look like? Not the Christ of the high cathedrals of Europe. No! This is a sea-going Christ. A Christ who beckons without compass; he bids his dear followers put out to sea and trust the currents as the channel of God's will. Brendan testified that Christ himself was their Captain.

> One day an island appeared to them in the distance, like a cloud on the horizon, and St. Brendan said to them: "My sons, do you recognize that island?" They answered that they did not. "Well, I recognize it. This is the island on which we celebrated Maundy Thursday last year, where our good steward lives." Then the monks were filled with joy and began to row as quickly as they could. When the man of God saw this, he said: "Don't row so hard, or you will exhaust yourselves. Is almighty God not the helmsman and captain of our ship? Do not strain yourselves, since he guides us where he will."

Christ leads Brendan forward, encircling him with love when the seas are stormy and he cannot find his way. Brendan found that Christ provides for all that is necessary on the journey.

> God, bless to me this day,
> God bless to me this night;
> Bless, O bless, Thou God of grace,
> Each day and hour of my life;
> > Bless, O bless, Thou God of grace,
> > Each day and hour of my life.

> God, bless the pathway on which I go,
> God, bless the earth that is beneath my sole;
> Bless, O God, and give to me Thy love,
> O God of gods, bless my rest and my repose;
> > Bless, O God, and give to me Thy love,
> > And bless, O God of gods, my repose.

SEEKING THE UNFINISHED ASSIGNMENT

Brendan called on God to bless him on his long, wandering journey. But why did he and his companions trust God? Because they knew Christ, God's Son, was the only pilot of their little coracle. It didn't matter whether the skies were overcast or clear, whether they could plot their course or not, because Christ was their Captain. His presence encircled them.

> Jesu! Only-begotten Son and Lamb of God the Father,
> Thou didst give the wine-blood of Thy body to buy me
>   from the grave.
> My Christ! my Christ! my shield, my encircler,
> Each day, each night, each light, each dark;
> My Christ! my Christ! my Shield, my encircler,
> Each day, each night, each light, each dark.
>
> Be near me, uphold me, my treasure, my triumph,
> In my lying, in my standing, in my watching, in my
>   sleeping,
> Jesu, Son of Mary! my helper, my encircler,
> Jesu, Son of David! my strength everlasting;
> Jesu, Son of Mary! my helper, my encircler,
> Jesu, Son of David! my strength everlasting.

These saints had a great imperative; Jesus' simple command, "Come, follow me" (Matthew 4:19). Though they didn't know where their Captain would lead them, they weren't concerned. In effect, the peregrini said, "We will follow God. If he takes us to Spain, fine. If Gaul, fine. Let us throw away the compass, for we have no need to know where we are. We are following Christ, and he guides our coracle. We seek the center of his will; everything else is just geography."

The peregrini set their eyes on Christ, not on their sails. God
sent the wind that directed their future. God was not so much
the "God of where they had been" as the "God of where they
were going." Like the rest of us, they knew they had only so
long to live, so they measured their days by trusting the remain-
der of their lives to "the God of what's left."

"We must measure our days," as Psalms 90:12 informs us,
"so that we may apply our hearts to wisdom" (KJV). We must be
wise in our present service, believing the Father, Son and Spirit
will direct our tomorrows. Like the peregrini, we need to understand that our pilgrimage will be finished when God says so.
Whether we know it or not, our life truly is a voyage. Hopefully
it's a voyage of following Christ in long, wandering prayer.

We say that we are committed to following Christ wherever
he leads. But the truth is that when Christ doesn't reveal where
we're going, we get antsy. To be happy, we've got to know our
destination. Rather than tarrying in prayer, we make plans for
ourselves. We make secondary plans in case our primary plans
don't work out. We make tertiary plans in case our secondary
plans don't work out. The very notion that God hold our plans
and that we get there only by trusting scares us to death.

The following Celtic prayer witnesses to the spirit of the
peregrini, who felt God could be trusted for both the voyage
and the destiny.

HELMSMAN: Blest be the boat.

CREW: God the Father bless her.

HELMSMAN: Blest be the boat.

CREW: God the Son bless her.

HELMSMAN: Blest be the boat.

CREW:	God the Spirit bless her.
ALL:	God the Father, God the Son, God the Spirit, Bless the boat.
HELMSMAN:	What can befall you And God the Father with you?
CREW:	No harm can befall us.
HELMSMAN:	What can befall you And God the Son with you?
CREW:	No harm can befall us.
HELMSMAN:	What can befall you And God the Spirit with you?
CREW:	No harm can befall us.
ALL:	God the Father, God the Son, God the Spirit, With us eternally.
HELMSMAN:	What can cause you anxiety And the God of the elements over you?
CREW:	No anxiety can be ours.
HELMSMAN:	What can cause you anxiety And the King of the elements over you?
CREW:	No anxiety can be ours.
HELMSMAN:	What can cause you anxiety And the Spirit of the elements over you?
HELMSMAN:	No anxiety can be ours.

ALL: The God of the elements,
                     The King of the elements,
                     The Spirit of the elements,
                     Close over us,
                     Ever eternally.

Why did they pray, "Bless be the boat"? Why didn't the peregrini pray, "God bless us. Give us journey mercies. Protect us
as we travel"? Because life is the journey. The peregrini said, in
effect, "On earth, it's on the journey we must serve. Our ultimate destination lies on the other side of death, so we aren't
concerned about it." The peregrini knew not whether their lives
would end at sea or on an island, but the end of it was out of
their hands. If they were martyred or blessed, the end was still
the same, they remained in God's will. There is a magnificent
sense of contentment in the way of the pilgrim, a contentment
that we too can share. The blessing for the journey rises from
the *Carmina Gadelica*.

> I set the keeping of Christ about thee,
> I send the guarding of God with thee.
> To possess thee, to protect thee
> From drowning, from danger, from loss,
>   From drowning, from danger, from loss.
> The Gospel of the God of grace
> Be from thy summit to thy soul;
> The Gospel of Christ, King of salvation,
> Be as a mantle to thy body,
>   Be as a mantle to thy body.
> Nor drowned be thou at sea,

Nor slain be thou on land,
Nor o'erborne be thou by man,
Nor undone be thou by woman,
   Nor undone be thou by woman!

THE END OF THE JOURNEY

As they journeyed, the peregrini learned to depend on God in a manner that most of us never experience. Although we live complacent lives of relative luxury, they blazed trails for Christ through an unfriendly and hostile world. We grow stagnant and struggle with short prayers, but they experienced life-changing growth through long, wandering prayer. These Celtic stories should lead us to the love of adventure. There are wonders awaiting all who pursue Christ throughout every area of our existence. Like them, we need to be willing to pray, "God, anywhere, anytime, bless this little boat, this voyage I am on. Give me travels in which I learn not necessarily where I am or how I'm getting on in the world, but the joy of sojourning that draws me into your presence. Help me to confidently sail with you into tomorrow, knowing that without you tomorrow has no significance but with you it holds no threat."

Of course, one of our tomorrows is going to will take us to the gates of death. We can prepare ourselves for this final journey by walking with a fellow pilgrim who is dying, offering our departing friends our prayer as a natural bridge in their final approach to God. Regarding this, Penelope Wilcock says:

To accompany other people, along with their loved ones, up to the gate of death is to enter Holy Ground. To stand in an awesome place where the wind of the Spirit blows;

to encounter peace and grief, insight, intimacy and pain on a level not found in ordinary living. By the side of the dying we learn stillness, waiting, simply being; the arts of quietness and keeping watch, prayer beyond words.

At death long, wandering prayer on earth finally reaches its end. It's time to put away the coracles, shred the sails, burn the oars and settle into the fullness of the presence we once only sought but now fully embrace. The union *we* tried to claim at last claims us. Our restlessness is over. The compass is discarded. The voyage ends. Then Christ, who at other times seemed so distant, says to us loud and clear, "Well done thou good and faithful servant."

LONG WANDERING PRAYER

To enter this brief self-study on prayer, it is important that you cast off all notions of prayers that are prayed in one position or in any fixed state of mind. See yourself in motion as in walking or driving, then apply this brief definition to all of life: *You are on a pilgrimage, and even as you sojourn—while walking or traveling in any manner—you are talking to God.* Yesterday informs your "in motion" prayers, tomorrow looms with intimidation that keeps you from knowing exactly what you must ask for and, therefore, today is the altar of informed prayer. Your prayer might go something like this:

Father of all humankind, who keeps my journey and marks the horizon of my destiny, love me through my journey toward tomorrow.

Son of God, leader and keeper of the maps, show me not

the whole road at once, but give me the distance to be gained in single steps.

Spirit of God, who holds my inner compass, may your presence on the journey awaken trust within me when I don't know what lies around the bend.

God bless to me this day, then I shall make my journey by sunlight and know the way.

Christ, bless to me this uncertain step, then I shall find the step more certain.

Spirit, bless to me this lonely moment, then I shall not be alone.

O Three-in-One, do guard my steps.

Travel with me God,
and I shall travel with the darkness at my back and the Sunlight on my face.

Travel with me Christ.
Then I shall mute the thunder,
and walk through lightning unafraid.

Travel with me Holy Spirit,
and my solo anthem shall have accompaniment through-out the journey.

I am coming to you O Three-in-One.
One day at a time,
one hour at a time,
one step at a time.

Amen.

Using the above Prayer of the Wayfarer, improvise your own lines:

Father of all humankind, who keeps my journey and marks the horizon as my destiny,

Son of God, leader and keeper of the maps, show me not the whole road at once, but give me

Spirit of God, may your presence on the journey always inform my need to

God bless to me this day, then I shall

Christ, bless to me this uncertain step, then I shall

Spirit, bless to me this lonely moment, then I shall

O Three-in-One do guard my steps,

Travel with me God,
and I shall

Travel with me Christ.
Then I shall

Travel with me Holy Spirit,
and

I am coming to you, O Three-in-One.
One day at a time,
one hour at a time,
one step at a time.

Amen.

Turn but a stone and an angel moves.

GEORGE MACDONALD

Heaven opened wide
Her ever-during gates, harmonious sound
On golden hinges moving, to let forth
The King of Glory, in his powerful Word
And Spirit coming to create new worlds.

JOHN MILTON, *PARADISE LOST*

Fresh fields and woods! the Earth's fair face,
God's foot-stool, and man's dwelling-place.

HENRY VAUGHAN, "THE RETIREMENT"

4

NATURE PRAYER

Poetry and Praise in Ordinary Life

In the concluding years of the nineteenth century, Alexander Carmichael gathered vast amounts of Celtic psalms, hymns and poetry under the title of *Carmina Gadelica*. Esther de Waal popularized these hymns and poems in her wonderfully inspirational *Celtic Way of Prayer*. It is not possible to understand these hymns without understanding how central the bard or poet was in the pre-Christian culture. The Druids—the wise men and priests and literary leaders of the Celts—were above all poets. They loved the everyday occurrences of their outdoor world; all that they saw became song and praise. But at the heart of their poems of praise were the miracles of ordinary life. In this simple devotion they were not unlike Sara Teasdale, for example, who observed:

> There will come soft rains,
> and the smell of ground
> and the swallows circling
> with a shimmering sound.

The Druids would have understood this simple celebration of rain.

The Celtic songs of religious spontaneity arose from ordinary life—the poetry and psalms of the *Carmina Gadelica*. In this exotic, folksy soil, we can let our own need to praise God take root. For here we see our love of all God created distilled into the pure praise of God himself. The nonliturgical lives of the Celts were rooted in the now. They believed that life should be lived in the moment. *Now* is our only guaranteed moment! Only in the present is it possible to pray. Try to put devotion anywhere else and it dies.

But devotion lives gloriously in Celtic praise. For them, the world of nature is far more than can be observed. It's where mere mortals become God's servants of praise. The Celts were Franciscan before there was a St. Francis. An old Gaelic woman illustrates this for us:

> My mother would be asking us to sing our morning song to God—as Mary's lark was singing it up in the clouds, and as Christ's mavis (*smeorach Chriosda*) was singing it yonder in the tree, giving glory to the God of the creatures (*dia nan dúl*) for the repose of the night, for the light of the day, and for the joy of life. She would tell us that every creature on the earth here below and in the ocean beneath and in the air above was giving glory to the great God of the creatures and the worlds, of the virtues and the blessings and would we be dumb! My dear mother reared her children in food and clothing, in love and charity. My heart loves the earth in which my beloved mother rests.

All Celtic worship sounds high praise to the God of the outdoors. When Brendan O'Malley composed his *Celtic Primer,* he included the natural force of "creature praise" that lies at the heart of Celtic worship. Unlike much church liturgy, Leslie Richards saw the Holy Spirit as the great *outdoor* Paraclete:

> Infinite and wise is God,
> The God who does not reveal
> The mysteries of his little insects,
> And his minutest creations
> That our eyes cannot see.
> Wise and infinite is the God
> who does not reveal
> The mysteries of his worlds and constellations,
> And his greatest creations
> That our imaginations cannot grasp.
> And because we cannot see,
> Because we cannot understand,
> Because we cannot grasp
> All his mysteries
> We can but marvel,
> And muse,
> And humbly bow to worship Him.

O'Malley enlarges the thought: "When the true shepherd speaks, and man hears him, the heart burns within, the flesh trembles, the mind lights like a candle, the conscience ferments like wine in a crock, and the will bows to the truth, and that small, powerful, heavenly voice raises up the dead from his own grave to live, to don the crown, and wonderfully changes the whole of life to live like the Lamb of God."

This uncanny and earthy way of speaking of the Holy Spirit

helps us see the Spirit flowing naturally through all of life, and therefore permeating the worship of the church.

This, God sustaining creation and his power being evident within creation, is why Columba said that to know the Creator you must seek him through creation. Indeed, Brendan went so far as to say, "The Eucharist is a concentrate of God's presence in all things." Bread and wine, everyday elements, can convey God's grace to us.

The God of presence must be welcomed into our hearts as God of the present. There are three things we might discover from the Celtic model: First, Christians who are close to nature can see the Maker in the things he has made. Second, once we have found evidence of the Creator in nature—our praise erupts spontaneously. Third, the overwhelming beauty of our Creator naturally evokes praise in poetry.

There is an early Irish prayer that fully demonstrates Christ Almighty's presence throughout creation. In this passage, the worshiper offers back to the Son of God all the natural world where he may be found.

> I offer Thee
> Every wave that ever moved,
> Every heart that ever loved,
> Thee, my Father's Well-Beloved.
> Dear Lord.
>
> Every River Dashing,
> Every lightning flashing,
> Like the angel's sword.
> Benedicimus Te!

I offer Thee Every Cloud that ever swept
O'er the skies and broke and wept
In rain, and with the flowerlets slept.
My King.

Each communicant praying,
Every angel staying
Before Thy throne to sing.
Adoramus Te!

I offer Thee
Every flake of virgin snow,
Every spring of earth below,
Every human joy and woe,
My love!

O Lord! And all the glorious
Self o'er death victorious,
Throned in Heaven above.
Glorificamus Te!

There is a fourth-century Eucharistic prayer that demonstrates the sovereignty of Christ throughout all creation. Although this prayer does not use the word *Christ* as the agent of creation, it does confess that all of it was done through Christ.

You appointed the sun in heaven to begin the day and the moon to begin the night, and you inscribed the chorus of the stars in heaven to the praise of your magnificence.

You made water for drinking and cleansing, life-giving air for breathing in and out, and for the production of sound through the tongue striking the air, and for hearing which is aided by it to receive the speech which falls upon it.

You made fire for comfort in darkness, for supplying our need, that we should be warmed and given light by it.

You divided the ocean from the land, and made the one navigable, the other fit to be trodden by our feet; you filled it with creatures small and great, tame and wild; you wove it a crown of varied plants and herbs, you beautified it with flowers and enriched it with seeds.

You constructed the abyss and set a great covering on it, the piled-up seas of salt water, and surrounded it with gates of finest sand; now you raise it with winds to the height of the mountains, now you level it to a plain; now you drive it to fury with a storm, now you soothe it with a calm, so that it gives an easy journey to travelers in ships.

You girdled the world that was made by you through Christ and flooded it with torrents, you watered it with ever-flowing springs and bound it round with mountains as an unshakeable and most safe seat for the earth.

For you filled the world and adorned it with sweet smelling and healing herbs, with many different living things, strong and weak, for food and for work, tame and wild, with hissing of reptiles, with the cries of varied birds, the cycles of the years, the numbers of months and days, the order of the seasons, the course of rain-bearing clouds for the production of fruits and the creation of living things, a stable for the winds that blow at your command, the multitude of plants and herbs.

God the Father is calling us to meet God the Son in the midst of his creation, all the while remembering our own special place in it as well (Genesis 1:26-30). And we, along with all of creation, have been honored by the incarnation of our Lord, who took upon himself the form of a creature (John 1).

GOD'S GLORY REFLECTED IN NATURE

The Celts understood that nature is the matrix into which the Christian gospel came. One Celtic hero who illustrates this truth is Brigit (born A.D. 452). The life of Brigit is admittedly filled with myth and legend. But Seán Ó Duinn has managed to demythologize her and at the same time allow her to remain in the center of Celtic natural theology. Brigit personally embodies the Celtic love of nature. The dew of a May morning, for example, had a special place in the hearts of the Irish, and Brigit became the holy saint of the simple world of dew and rain.

> The fair maid who,
> the first of May,
> goes to the field
> at break of day,
> And washes in the dew
> from the Hawthorn tree,
> will ever after handsome be.

In May, it was a custom in Derbyshire for the fair young maidens to lay a sheet on the ground to collect the dew of the night and wash themselves with it the following morning to increase their beauty. They also used it to wash the children to give them special cleansing power for their growing years. Some Celts around Cork believed that linen soaked with the dew of May retained a curative and cleansing power all year long.

It's difficult to separate myth from reality in Brigit's life. But Ó Duinn helps us understand that stripped of lore and legend, she was a holy woman who loved God and served his people. She loved Christ *and* the world God made. The gospel did spread in Celtic lands during her life, and through her simple ministry many Celts were converted to Christianity. Thus she became the matron saint of Ireland and was woven into the fabric of their worship and prayer. And in Brigit many modern Celts can still hear God's pristine call issuing from the hills and woodlands and streams of Ireland.

In our day people such as the environmentalist Rachel Carson and the writer Annie Dillard call on us to see the mysterious power of nature and let its wonders be collected in our souls. If we heed this call, we will spontaneously praise the triune God who is Maker of heaven and earth. Dillard and Carson call us to a holistic view of God's good creation. Scripture clearly declares, "The earth is the LORD's, and the fulness thereof" (Psalm 24:1 KJV). And we have been given a mandate to care for God's property (Genesis 2:15). If we allow our environment to deteriorate, not only will we have disobeyed God but humans will have no place to live and worship.

The Celts were far less sophisticated than modern environmentalists and theologians, but in their simple faith their esteem for God and his creation took root in the ancient Celtic soil. Nature, for them, moved through a recurring cycle around a spinning clock, defining not just springtime and harvest but also the entire Christian calendar.

Honey under ground
Silverweed of spring.
Honey and condiment
Whisked whey of summer.
Honey and fruitage
Carrot of autumn.
Nuts of winter
Between Feast of Andrew
And Christmastide.

Here rings two calendars: that of the church and that by which the birds nested and the mountains delivered their spring waters to the valleys. In their praise of nature the Celts sometimes sound as though they have confused it with God, but follow their nature praise far enough and you will find it is really directed to God. Never did the sun rise but what the Celts saw the triune God in the light. Alexander Carmichael wrote:

Old men in the Isles still uncover their heads when they first see the sun on coming out in the morning. They hum a hymn not easily caught up and not easily got from them. One such reciter said, "There was a man in Arasaig, and he was extremely old, and he would make adoration to the sun and to the moon and to the stars. When the sun would rise on the tops of the peaks he would put off his head covering and he would bow his head, giving glory to the great God of life for the glory of the sun and the goodness of its light, to the children of men and to the animals of the world. When the sun set in the western ocean, the old man would again take off his head covering, and he would bow his head to the ground and say:

I am in hope in its proper time,

That the great and gracious God

Will not put out for me the light of grace

Even as thou dost leave me this night.

The old man said that he had learned this from his father and the old men of the village when he was a small
child."

It is difficult to cut the sun and the moon off from the human
soul. Christians relate to nature just as much as other religious
people do. We bind spring to Easter and the resurrection to
sunrise. Try as we might, we cannot imagine Christ rising from
the dead in the evening. Maundy Thursday is the stuff of darkness, and starlight marks Christmas Eve. The difference is that
modern Christians merely paste nature over supernature, making it mere scenery. We so separate nature and faith that it seems
the worship of the church would be essentially unchanged if
creation ceased to exist. Not so with the Celts (or the Bible).

Pristine nature is refreshingly simple yet mysterious. It leads
the heart to unadulterated worship. Often, it seems, humanly
created formulas overlay worship with a heavy institutionalism
that smothers the simple life of the church. As one Irish church-
man said: "I love the Irish Catholic church—when it is left
alone." Sever its roots and its power is gone. The Irish church
owes its very uniqueness—its freshness—to its Celtic roots.

We desperately need to return to the power of our Creator
God. But we can never fully appreciate the Creator's presence in
the natural world until we know his inner presence. The Creator and the Redeemer are one and the same. Only those who
know and adore the cross of their "fairest Lord Jesus" can ap-

preciate the fact that he is "Maker of heaven and earth." Exhib-
iting this deeper knowledge of the redeeming Creator, Manchán
the monk, in describing the ideal monastery, wrote:

> I wish, O Son of the living God, eternal ancient King, for a
> hidden little hut in the wilderness that it might be my
> dwelling. All-grey shallow water beside it, a clear pool to
> wash away sins through the grace of the Holy Spirit. A
> beautiful wood close by, surrounding it on every side, for
> the nurture of many-voiced birds, for shelter to hide them.

Eire, the goddess who gave her name to pre-Christian
Ireland—Eire's Land—was the great mother god who created
harvest and orchards, filled the streams with fish, and the forests with deer. Her benevolence was born of the desire to see
the people of her land prosper. Her fecundity added to the
Celtic Christian understanding of both the creativity and prov-
idence of God. The praise that the pre-Christian Celts had as-
cribed to Eire was magnified when they directed it to the Trinity,
as evidenced by this eighth-century prayer:

> Let us pray to God the Father, God the Son
> and to God the Holy Spirit
> Whose infinite greatness
> Enfolds the whole world,
> In persons three and one,
> In essence simple and triune,
> Sustaining the earth above the waters,
> Hanging the upper air with stars,
> That he may be favorable to sinners
> Who righteously justifies all who err,

Who ever-living lives.

May God be blessed for ages. Amen.

It seems that God so filled the pre-Christian Celtic spirit with the love of creation that when they met Christ that love naturally spilled over into their Christian worship. Everywhere they looked, they saw the creative love and almighty nature of the holy Trinity.

I believe the Celts had this right. I have come late to this beautiful, ancient truth. I first felt its power, I believe, in the writings of Esther de Waal, which I read in 1999. But by the time I had actually visited Iona in 2005, I was convinced that we who serve an entirely indoor God have lost a great part of our faith. We must break through the cold, hard walls our institutionalized worship and reach for the soft, warm reality of God that is found out of doors. It is impossible to imprison God within walls of a church and yet claim that Christianity brings light, growth and life. We need to open the windows of our souls to admit God's creative energy.

Our inside God is too small. We need to view him through the universe he created. Then he will be elevated to his exalted place. Just as God asked Job, he asks us:

Do you know how God controls the clouds
    and makes his lightning flash?
Do you know how the clouds hang poised,
        those wonders of him who is perfect in knowledge?
(Job 37:15-16 NIV)

A supersized God makes us aware of our smallness and our humble place in the universe. But in order to see him, we must give up our addiction to electronic media. Once we have seen the God of Yosemite and the Everglades, we will be better able to celebrate his awesome reality and our hearts will overflow with praise. Cognizant of God's majesty, we will subsequently and spontaneously confess our need.

There is a song sung at Christmas by the Celts. It is sung by six souls hidden beneath a sheet so they appear to be a tup (or ram), complete with a ram's head on the front of the twelve legged ram. But it is a song of pleading humility, begging entrance from the God who made the tup, in the first place:

> There is a little tup,
> He's standing at your door;
> And if you'll have 'im in, Sir,
> He'll please you more and more.

This is perhaps the real meaning of all prayer. God is great, and we are greatly in need. When we find his all-sufficient mercy, we become new creations and our relationship to God transformed. Then we truly become people of faith.

SATAN IN THE WORLD

Sometimes we have let nature swallow the supernatural, leading to ugliness and despair. Nature must not forget the Christ that died to redeem it from its great destroyer—Satan. For just as God is the Creator of all things, so Satan would destroy all that God has made. The Celts understood this and diligently worked to prevent an unredeemed earth from storming heaven. They believed that after dying on the cross, Jesus went to hell to fight the destroyer and set all of the captives free. Christ has successfully harrowed hell. Ó Duinn explains:

Basically, the *Plundering of Hell* is an expression of the eternal warfare between good and evil, light and darkness, God and Satan. The war occurs in all three spheres—heaven, earth and the underworld. St. Michael figures in all three areas: "and now war broke out in heaven, when Michael with his angels attacked the dragon. The dragon fought back with his angels, but they were defeated and driven out of heaven. The great dragon, the primeval serpent, known as the devil or Satan, who had deceived all the world, was hurled down to the earth and his angels were hurled down with him."

Satan failed, yet he continues to battle, hoping to make inroads within God's creation. And we who are redeemed have been given the Holy Spirit to withstand Satan's onslaught. Like the Celts, through trinitarian eyes we fight evil, embrace a holistic view of nature and praise our wondrous Creator.

THE GLORY OF CREATION EVOKES THE POETRY OF PRAISE

Christianity, unlike some religions, is an incarnational faith. That is, a person of one culture does not have to embrace another culture to be a follower of Christ. Just as the Son of God became a Jewish man, ate Jewish food, spoke Aramaic and wore sandals and a robe, a Chinese woman who becomes a Christian remains Chinese—retaining all of her native culture that does not stand against the Word of God. At times, the gospel clashes with aspects of a given culture, but it also gives new meaning to many traditional beliefs and practices. This is true of the Celts.

When the good news of Christ came to Ireland, the Celts

were already accustomed to thinking of at least some of their gods in semi-trinitarian terms. Ted Olsen explains: "A common theme throughout Celtic religion is triune gods—gods with three manifestations, gods who travel in threes, or gods with three heads." Thus, they were more naturally inclined to embrace the Christian Trinity (see chap. 2) than were other peoples. The pre-Christian Celts, in believing in that a natural force they called the *neart* (also *níurt* or *nìrt*), could see that God permeated nature with a very available power that humans could tap for their own use in navigating life. Many believed Christ offered them the *neart* as their own God-given power to do good.

> I rise today,
>> in the power's strength *[neart]*, invoking the Trinity,
>> believing in the threeness, confessing the oneness,
>> of creation's Creator.
>
> I rise today,
>> in the *[neart]* power of Christ's birth and baptism,
>> in the *[neart]* power of his crucifixion and burial,
>> in the *[neart]* power of his rising and ascending,
>> in the *[neart]* power of his descending and judging.

And in their prayers, they asked the triune God to strengthen them with the *neart*. The Christian understanding of creation pressed new meaning and significance into the Celtic view of the natural world. And under this new Christ-force, they responded to the Creator in praise.

This really should not surprise us. Something in the out-of-doors always moves us to ponder God's majesty. Indeed, "The heavens declare the glory of God; / the skies proclaim the work of his hands" (Psalm 19:1). It evokes art and poetry. The Celtic poets, artists and monks chose not to "hide" their works of praise in cathedrals or castles. They made galleries of forests, meadows and craggy islands, the very places that inspired them to create. Here lived their King. Here rose his altar. While Michelangelo painted heaven on the Sistine ceiling, the Celts, in song, set his throne in God's starry skies.

The Celtic faith has generated abstractions that haunt the eye. Their great artists created a linear form that defies the mind to find a beginning or end. These intriguing lines remind us of the eternal, triune God. Celtic art, like their worship, is unique. Their love for nature and the God who stood beneath, behind and above it issued in their sculpture, crafts, poetry and songs. Celtic singing and dancing and poetry was shaped by God as they found him revealed in nature and Scripture.

Like most of the ancients, Celts did not distinguish between the sacred and profane. They had a holistic worldview. For them, there was only one world, and that world included faith and reason seamlessly together. Thus Celtic art intertwined the natural and supernatural worlds. While they were a "God-intoxicated people," they "relished their humanity, their love of learning and of life."

The Celtic poets drew their images not from a cloistered world they had never seen but from within creation itself. Though the following Celtic prayer is not as ancient as some Celtic runes, it is a splendid example of their use of nature in art:

O star-like sun, O guiding light, O home of the planets,
O fiery-maned and marvelous one, O fertile, undulating
    fiery sea,
Forgive.

O fiery glow, O fiery flame of judgment,
Forgive.
O holy storyteller, holy scholar, O full of holy grace, of
  holy strength,
O overflowing, loving silent one, O generous and
  thunderous giver of gifts,
Forgive.
O rock-like warrior of a hundred hosts,
O fair-crowned one, O victorious, skilled in battle,
Forgive.

Celtic art was born of their love for creation on one hand and
praise of their Creator on the other. No matter the subject of their
art, all glory was given to God. The following thirteenth century
poem, "The Loves of Taliesin," extols the beauty of creation:

The beauty of summer, its days long and slow,
Beautiful too visiting the ones we love.
The beauty of flowers on the tops of fruit trees, . . .
Beautiful too the foam-mouth and slender steed.
The beauty of the garden when the leeks grow well,
Beautiful too the charlock in bloom.
The beauty of the horse in its leather halter,
Beautiful too keeping company with a king. . . .
The beauty of heather when it turns purple,
Beautiful too moorland for cattle.

Nevertheless, the poem, as is typical, concludes with praise of
God:

The beauty of the word which the Trinity speaks,
Beautiful too doing penance for sin.

But the loveliest of all is covenant
With God on the day of judgment.

Celtic creation prayer is not just the praise of nature. Ultimately it raises its voice in honor of the source of all nature, the holy Trinity. Columba's *Altus Prosator* reminds us that in the end of days all nature will bow to the Creator.

When Christ, the most high Lord, comes down from the
    heavens,
The brightest sign and standard of the Cross will shine
    forth.
The two principal lights being obscured,
The stars will fall to earth like the fruit of a fig tree
And the face of the world will be like the fire of a
    furnace. . . .
By the singing of hymns eagerly ringing out,
By thousands of angels rejoicing in holy dances,
And by the four living creatures full of eyes,
With the twenty-four joyful elders
Casting their crowns under the feet of the Lamb of God,
The Trinity is praised in eternal threefold exchanges.

CREATION AND CALVARY

God has told us that creation is good (Genesis 1). We can learn from the holistic Celts that there is no cleavage between the created world and the redeeming God. Creation and redemption go hand in hand. God has not forsaken his creation (Romans 8:19-20). Indeed, at the end of the age he will recreate the heavens and earth, wherein we creatures will praise him forevermore. Listen to the wonderful unity of creation and redemption in the ninth-century poet Thomas:

> Almighty Creator, it is you who have made the land and
> the sea. . . . The world cannot comprehend in song bright
> and melodious, even though the grass and the trees
> should sing, all your wonders, O true Lord! The Father
> created the world by a miracle; it is difficult to express its
> measure.
>
> Letters cannot contain it, letters cannot comprehend it.
> Jesus created for the hosts of Christendom, with miracles
> when he came, resurrection through his nature. He who
> made the wonder of the world will save us, has saved us.
> It is not too great a toil to praise the Trinity.

Many of us have cut ourselves off from the great outdoors—
God's good creation. We live in an artificial environment of concrete, steel, plastic and glass. We often move from air-condi-
tioned house to climate-controlled car through the concrete
jungle to the cubicle "farm" of the office or the numbing same-
ness of the megamall. We literally don't even stop to smell the
roses. No wonder we exhibit little creature praise!

Why not let the example of the Celts inspire us? We can begin in small ways by taking walks, planting flowers, enjoying
the melodious birds and peering at the twinkling stars. On
weekends we can honor our Creator by exploring a park or
swimming in a lake or hiking a nature trail. Shortly we may find
our lives of praise blossoming and our relationship to the triune
Creator God growing ever deeper and more solid.

Come then. Lift your eyes to your true home—the world.
Actively observe the glory of your primary address—this planet
whose children tell of a carpenter who lived and died outside.

Come praise the God who chose for you this third rock out from the sun to be the first temple of your worship. It is this God of Earth-day, that is the God of Good Friday—the God of creation, the God of Calvary!

NATURE PRAISE

For these exercises it is best to find an outdoor location, weather permitting, and allow the unhurried moments some extra time if needed. Nature praying, above all other forms, is best if it is not forced into a hurried agenda. I love to walk outside—often in my small garden—find a comfortable lawn swing, sit down, open my Bible and, sipping coffee or tea, drift into an unhurried attitude of devotion. It is good to open the Bible to some of the final chapters of Job, the nineteenth Psalm, the creation passage of Genesis or the intimate outdoor passages of the Song of Solomon, and begin to read—stopping periodically to lift your eyes to the greens and blues of this world, making a conscious attempt to let your prayers enter into a spirit of thanksgiving for all his goodness in creation.

These prayers are prayers of celebration and will have more of a praise feeling than a feeling of petition about them. Let your adoration follow in these three compelling steps.

Step 1. Begin with a passage celebrating the ordinary aspects of creature and creation.

> Father, Creator, here is my prayer.
> Christ, Creator, here is my prayer.
> Spirit, Creator, here is my prayer.
>
> Listen to this, Job;

stop and consider God's wonders.
Do you know how God controls the clouds
   and makes the lightening flash?
Do you know how the clouds hang poised,
   those wonders of him who is perfect in knowledge?
You who swelter in your clothes
   when the land lies hushed under the south wind,
can you join him in spreading out the skies,
   hard as a mirror of cast bronze? . . .
Now no one can look at the sun,
   bright as it is in the skies,
   after the wind has swept them clean.
Out of the north he comes in golden splendor;
   God comes in awesome majesty.
The Almighty is beyond our reach and exalted in power.
(Job 37:14-18, 21-23 NIV)

Step 2. Add to the fullness of your Scripture-prayer by praying one of the grand nature hymns.

I sing th' Almighty power of God,
That made the mountains rise,
That spread the flowing seas abroad,
And built the lofty skies.
I sing the wisdom that ordained
The sun to rule the day;
The moon shines full at God's command,
And all the stars obey.

I sing the goodness of the Lord,

Who filled the earth with food,
Who formed the creatures through the Word,
And then pronounced them good.
Lord, how thy wonders are displayed,
Wherever I turn my eye,
If I survey the ground I tread,
Or gaze upon the sky.

There's not a plant or flower below,
But makes Thy glories known,
And clouds arise, and tempests blow,
By order from thy throne;
While all that borrows life from Thee
Is ever in thy care,
And everywhere that man can be,
Thou, God, are present there. (Isaac Watts, 1715)

Step 3. Then finally compose your own nature praise by using
the text and the hymn in alternate and repeated progressions.

Do you know how God controls the clouds
    and make the lightening flash?

Lord, here I praise you for the ordinary sights that greet my vision:

Can you join him in spreading out the skies,
    hard as a mirror of cast bronze?

Lord, here I praise you for the skies framed for your imminent return:

Now no one can look at the sun,
    bright as it is in the skies,
    after the wind has swept them clean.
Out of the north he comes in golden splendor;
    God comes in awesome majesty.

Lord, here I praise you for the golden sun, and its warmth that keeps the world from dark, unending nights.

Father, who made the seas, I praise you.
Son, who walked on them, I praise you.
Spirit, engulfing me with tides of swelling adoration,
    I praise you.

Amen.

Lord, set me on the rampart.

Give me health enough to live to complete the dream.

St. Patrick

Uriel shall be at my feet,

Ariel shall be at my back,

Gabriel shall be at my head,

And Raphael shall be at my side.

from the Carmina Gadelica

5

LORICA PRAYER

Asking God for Protection

Life is a journey, and journeys are interim passages filled with uncertainties. Where there are journeys there is the certainty that we must do battle with the "slings and arrows of outrageous fortune." So the wise pilgrim carries a first-aid kit. The Christian sojourner begs for the shield of God to cover us from the rain of arrows. We are woundable by all the unexpected stones that cut and bruise, maim or kill. From obstetrician to mortician, our lives are filled with peril, and we dare not make the journey unprotected.

Naked on the field of battle, we cry out for God to clothe us in his armor.

Prayers for God's protection must be set in the context from which they are offered. Premodern people reckoned with plague and pestilence, and slavery and genocide. Even "innocent" colds often resulted in death. The ancients found few old people among them. Life was violent and short. But the Celts found much-needed solace in the *lorica*.

The *lorica* (Latin for breastplate) was a piece of armor that protects the heart. Much like the apostle Paul, Celts saw prayer as their breastpale—a protective layer of steely, spiritual defense. Paul wrote to the Ephesians:

> Finally, be strong in the Lord and in his mighty power. Put on the full armor of God so that you can take your stand against the devil's schemes. For our struggle is not against flesh and blood, but against the rulers, against the authorities, against the powers of this dark world and against the spiritual forces of evil in the heavenly realms. (Ephesians 6:10-12)

The loricae (plural) were entreaties that mattered greatly to the ancients. These were prayers of armor that wrapped Christians in God's safety. The lorica prayer kept fever and contagion at a distance. "Breastplate" praying was the hope-filled entreaty that made the dream of old age less risky. Tomorrow could be lived free of threat with God's protective armor.

In ancient times, every person had a favorite way of facing tomorrow. There were apothecaries and herbalists who could cook up a brew of forest herbs that might deal with this ailment or that disease. There were witches and warlocks whose incantations could cast out demons or curse an enemy.

Ancient peoples who became Christians, casting aside herbalists and shamans, saw nothing unusual in asking the triune God to protect them instead. They were, after all, part of God's advancing kingdom and if they ceased to live, God's work—in their corner of the kingdom—would go unfinished. Their prayers for protection were not "name it and claim it" or "health and wealth gospel" prayers. When prayed with the proper motives, the lorica to the Celts is genuine prayer. Celts did not ask God to give them life for their own sake. God's protection enabled them to prosper his kingdom. At heart the lorica says, God, only while I live can I serve you, so please protect and extend my life.

SELF-DENIAL AND THE GOD-CENTERED LIFE

Everything about Christianity teaches us self-denial. So much so that when we come to the point of praying for ourselves—even to get well—we are afraid that we might be doing something wrong! Some Christ followers don't feel very comfortable praying for their own well-being. But there is room for praying for our own good health within truly selfless intercession. We creatures pray for the Creator's protection that we might expand and enjoy his creation.

Praying for ourselves in any manner, however, may seem to some to be in conflict with Christ's call to deny ourself, take up our cross and follow him (Matthew 16:24). Perhaps this is why Mother Teresa forbade the nuns of her order to pray for themselves even when they were desperately ill. They could pray for other members of the Sisters of Charity but not for themselves. The Celts, though, could honestly maintain their self-denial while praying for the good state of their own well-being.

In context, a prayer for protection while gathering wood, let us say, might not be selfish if the wood collected was used to warm the house and allow the wood gatherers' families to live. In the rain-drenched, often cold and wintry lands of the Celts, a fire in the hearth signaled that all was well. Prayers such as Patrick's "Breastplate" reveal that we can cry out for the armor of God's protection as we seek to actively do his will.

Jesus was tempted by Satan to give in to a selfish agenda (see Matthew 4:1-11). In each case Jesus refused. Though he was very hungry, Jesus refused to make stones into bread. And he refused to avoid the cross by taking a short-cut to ownership of all the kingdoms of the world. In each case, Jesus refused self-aggrandizement. We too must beware of asking for things to fulfill selfish desires. On the other hand, a mother may pray, for example, for her own health so that she may care for her children. Her health is a key factor in the lives of others. Such is the motive behind lorica praying.

THE LORICA: INVOKING THE VICTOR

The lorica is found in the breastplate of Ephesians 6:13-18.

Therefore put on the full armor of God, so that when the day of evil comes, you may be able to stand your ground, and after you have done everything, to stand. Stand firm then, with the belt of truth buckled around your waist, with the *breastplate* of righteousness in place, and with your feet fitted with the readiness that comes from the gospel of peace. In addition to all this, take up the shield of faith, with which you can extinguish all the flaming arrows of the evil one. Take the helmet of salvation and the sword of the Spirit, which is the word of God. *And pray in the Spirit on all occasions with all kinds of prayers and requests.* With this in mind, be alert and always keep on praying for all the saints. (Emphasis added)

The armor of God protects us as we work in God's kingdom. And we are exhorted to "pray . . . all kinds of prayers and requests." The "gates of hell" cannot withstand the advance of

Christ's church (Matthew 16:18). But the church cannot advance into this battle without armor. Our success in the warfare depends on the lorica. We are soldiers and the enemy is real. Seán Ó Duinn informs us that the Celts had "a highly militaristic conception of Christian life which would have to some extent been characteristic of the early church. The forces of evil and death were very real. The Christian was a soldier who by his baptism had undertaken a lifelong battle against these forces."

This talk of spiritual battle may seem quite alien to many of us. But it was very real to the Celts. And clothing themselves with the lorica was quite consistent with the biblical worldview. In reality, we must go toe-to-toe with the devil in the name of Christ. In a fifteenth-century retelling of Christ's harrowing of hell, Satan

> realises that Christ derives his power from God and that if Christ were to sin he would lose this power, sends his demons to tempt Christ to sin. They come one by one to tempt him and they are personified as the seven deadly sins. When they get back, Satan questions them individually about how they got on and the seven have to admit sadly that they did not succeed in tempting Christ. Satan sends them away in disgust and tries to fortify hell as best he can against attack. Christ comes along however and liberates the captives and goes away leaving Satan tied to a pillar in the depths of hell.

Satan is still active and powerful in our world, and as we advance on his domain, he does his best to set up roadblocks against our advance. Sickness, pestilence and enemies are all a part of his arsenal. But through breastplate prayers, we are protected.

PRAYING FOR PROTECTION TO SERVE
GOD'S AGENDA

In order to remain true to Christ, who is infinitely more power-ful than Satan, we must learn what God is doing in the world. Then, by the power of the Spirit, we can strive to follow Christ by echoing his example in the world. Columbanus reflects this understanding in his encouragement to his fellow sailors:

> The tempests howl, the storms dismay,
> But manly strength can win the day.
> Heave, lads, and let the echoes ring.

> For clouds and squalls will soon pass on,
> And victory lie with work well done.
> Heave, lads, and let the echoes ring.

> The King of virtues vowed a prize,
> For him who wins, for him who tries,
> Think, lads, of Christ and echo him.

Columbanus asks for protection from the storm and for the strength to heave on the oars in order that his sailors may echo Christ. Once they successfully landed, they brought the gospel to the Germans. We too must "echo Christ" in the world. Again, though, we must check our motives: will our prayers enable us to enter greater arenas of service for God? Or are we more con-cerned about our own interests rather than those of others? When we offer our pilgrimage to God, we pray the lorica. It is important for us to be strong enough to complete our pilgrim-age for God's own purposes.

When we see ourselves as pilgrims, it will be easier for us to pray our own lorica, like "The Power of God" from Patrick's

"Breastplate." This is merely a matter of pluralizing Patrick's first person lorica.

> May the way of God direct us,
> May the shield of God defend us,
> May the host of God guard us against snares of evil
> and the temptations of the world.

When you deny yourself—when you center completely on Christ—you become incapable of praying selfishly.

PROTECT ME SO I CAN DO A GOOD JOB FOR YOU

There are three unselfish loricae.

- Let me live to complete the dream I have for you, God.
- Let me live until my season of worship is complete.
- Let me live long enough to bear a saving word to those outside of your grace.

Let's consider these one at a time.

Let me live to complete the dream. In a time of deep trouble, Patrick prayed, "I was like a stone lying in the deepest mire; and then, he who is mighty came, and, in his mercy, raised me up. He most truly raised me on high and set me on top of the rampart." In effect he prayed, "Lord, set me on the rampart. Give me health required so I may live to complete the dream."

In the midst of any misfortune that confronts you, make Patrick's prayer your own, "Lord, let me live to complete the dream." If ever there was a saint who felt the burden of the calling of God, it was Patrick. So much of Ireland needed to be converted. Men and women were without Christ, and Patrick took their spiritual fortunes most seriously. He cried out to live, not to avoid death, but to complete the winning of Ireland to

Christ. God granted him life and he left behind him an Ireland that served the triune God.

But even more than his prayers for his own longevity, Patrick passionately desired that his work for Christ would live on in the lives of others who would take the gospel from Ireland to Scotland and then to all of Europe.

Let me live until my season of worship is complete. Here is what the early church historian Bede said of Alban (the first British martyr, of the third or fourth century): "For Christ's sake, [Alban] bore the most horrible torments patiently and gladly, and . . . the judge saw that no torture could break him or make him renounce the *worship* of Christ."

Here's an interesting notion for praying the lorica. Not only do we have a task to be done but, like Alban, we also have a worship to complete. We pray and we seek after God so that our adoration of him will find its fullest expression. Often those who are seriously ill or in great pain find it difficult to praise God. In fact, when pain reaches its zenith almost all concord between God and his beloved child dies. Therefore the prayer is reasonable: *I have worship I want to complete. I want to rise in the morning to praise you and to go to bed at night in full strength to praise you in full force.* So our lorica becomes: Let me live. Protect my life until my season of worship is completed.

Let me live long enough to bear a saving word to those outside of your grace. The ancient Celts of the British Isles, beginning with Patrick, were very evangelistic. During this time the church experienced a surge of mission, a great desire to bring the good news of Christ to the whole world. Thus the Celtic message moved from Ireland to the Hebrides, then to England and finally across Europe.

We need this vision. There are still people who do not know Christ and will not spend eternity with God. Like the Celts, we are ambassadors for Christ, and we therefore bear a saving word for the world. It is reasonable to pray for God's protection that we might point the way to Christ to those who are outside of God's grace.

FROM GENERAL TO SPECIFIC

Scripture encourages us to pray very specifically. After all, God numbers the hairs on our head (Matthew 10:30)—now that's specific! Let's look at "The Breastplate of Laidcenn" to see how specific the Celts could get in their prayers.

O God, defend me everywhere
With your impregnable power and protection.
Deliver all my mortal limbs,
Guarding each with your protective shield,
So the foul demons shall not hurl their darts
Into my side, as is their wont.

Deliver my skull, hair-covered head, and eyes,
Mouth, tongue, teeth, and nostrils,
Neck, breast, side, and limbs,
Joints, fat, and two hands.

Be a helmet of safety to my head,
To my crown covered with hair,
To my forehead, eyes, and triform brain,
To snout, lip, face, and temple.

To my chin, beard, eyebrows, ears,
Chaps, cheeks, septum, nostrils,

Pupils, irises, eyelids, and the like,
To gums, breath, jaws, gullet.

Protect my spine and ribs and their joints,
Back, ridge, and sinews with their bones;
Protect my skin and blood with kidneys,
The area of the buttocks, nates with thighs.
Protect my hams, calves, femurs,
Houghs and knees with knee-joints;
Protect my ankles and shins and heels,
Shanks, feet with their soles.

Protect my toes growing together,
With the tips of the toes and twice five nails;
Protect my breast, collarbone and small breast,
Nipples, stomach, and navel.

Protect the whole of me with my five senses,
Together with the ten created orifices,
So that from soles of feet to crown of head
I shall not sicken in any organ inside or out.

The saints who prayed this breastplate prayer saw the clear relationship between health and the business of God. The specificity is breathtaking! Though not so concerned about the body, Patrick's "Breastplate" is specific about other dangers:

I rise today:
in the power of Christ's birth and baptism,
in the power of his crucifixion and burial,
in the power of his rising and ascending,
in the power of his descending and judging.
Around me I gather today all these powers:

against every cruel and merciless force
to attack my body and soul,
against the charms of false prophets,
the black laws of paganism,
the false laws of heretics,
the deceptions of idolatry,
against spells cast by women, smiths, and druids,
and all unlawful knowledge
that harms the body and soul.
May Christ protect me today:
against poison and burning,
against drowning and wounding
so that I may have abundant reward.

As long as the lorica is prayed daily, the believer can go boldly into the world to do a mighty work for God. The lorica can become a significant part of our life as we serve others and expand God's kingdom on earth. When prayer becomes our way of life, we achieve the fullest kind of life in fellowship with God.

REAL-LIFE EXAMPLES

A woman I knew had heart disease and her future was bleak. Being on a transplant list gave her hope, but her hope dwindled with each passing day as her condition deteriorated. Finally, all hope was gone. She was completely inert and confined to a bed; only the tubes and oxygen mask kept her alive. The family was called in because her doctor determined she would be gone in a matter of hours. I too was called to administer an evangelical offering of last rites—a word of prayer—for the final crossing.

When I was alone with her, I prayed for God to heal her and for her to receive the donor heart she so desperately needed, despite the fact that it seemed an utterly hopeless situation. That night, eighty miles from where the woman lay, a young man was tragically killed in a motorcycle accident. His heart was flown to the woman's hospital and a team of surgeons attended our dying friend. The woman, bright and alive, was back in church six weeks later. She walked confidently to the pulpit and gave her testimony.

The lorica is a wonderful garment—a breastplate of hope for the darkest nights of our lives.

While on a hunting trip, one of my good friends had a heart attack far from home. He drove himself an agonizing seventy miles to a hospital, checked in and immediately underwent quadruple bypass surgery. He was, in his own opinion, a goner. But in the succeeding weeks of his recuperation, he began to pray Psalm 116 as his lorica.

> I love the LORD, for he heard my voice;
>   he heard my cry for mercy.
> Because he turned his ear to me,
>   I will call on him as long as I live.
> The cords of death entangled me,
>   the anguish of the grave came upon me;
>   I was overcome by trouble and sorrow.
> Then I called upon the name of the LORD:
>   "O LORD, save me!'
> The LORD is gracious and righteous;
>   our God is full of compassion.
> The LORD protects the simplehearted;

when I was in great need, he saved me.
Be at rest once more, O my soul,
   for the LORD has been good to you.
For you, O LORD, have delivered my soul from death.
   my eyes from tears,
   my feet from stumbling,
That I may walk before the LORD
   in the land of the living. (Psalm 116:1-9 NIV)

To keep this breastplate security close at hand, my friend memorized this psalm. Now he can pray it as often as he wishes without even opening his Bible. We would do well to do the same with the passages that mean the most to us.

PROTECTIVE BENEDICTION

A protective benediction is a form of Scripture praying most often prayed at the end of the day. The force of the Trinity is invoked in this benediction:

> The Three that are the oldest, the Three that are youngest, the Three that are strongest in the city of glory—the Father, Son and Holy Spirit—may they be protecting me, saving me, from tonight until a year from tonight and tonight itself.

These wonderful benedictions become a form of direct, powerful and effective Scripture praying.

> The LORD bless thee, and keep thee.
> The LORD make his face shine upon thee, and be gracious unto thee:
> The LORD lift up his countenance upon thee, and give thee peace. (Numbers 6:24-26 KJV)

The following forceful words of Jude can be used to bless all of our friends in Christ:

> To him who is able to keep you from falling and to present you before his glorious presence without fault and with great joy—to the only God our Savior be glory, majesty, power and authority, through Jesus Christ our Lord, before all ages, now and forevermore! Amen. (Jude 24-25 NIV)

In praying such Scripture, bringing glory to God is primary, allowing the Holy Spirit to work in our lives as a spiritual force from God that provides a strong holiness for our weak obedience and glorious health for our frailty.

In the meantime put on the breastplate of righteousness—the lorica. Let your prayer for protection offer you the full power of the Trinity.

> I make this bed tonight (today) in the name of the Father, the Son and the Holy Spirit, in the name of the night in which we were conceived, in the name of the day on which we were baptized, in the name of every saint and every apostle in heaven.

PRAYING THE LORICA TODAY

The lorica prayer was not just a good idea for ancient people; we too need God's protection. Modern medical and technological advances tend to push God to the periphery of life, diluting our understanding that we are completely dependent on God. It is proper and right to seek God's protection. He purifies, heals and gives us a future. And with the health he gives, we rise to take care of the business of God. When our lives are centered on Christ, we beg his protection that we may complete our dream, live until our worship is complete, and bear a saving word to all of those outside of God's grace. Thus, along with the Celts, we look to God and pray:

> Alone with none but thee, my God,
> I journey on my way;
> What need I fear, when thou art near,
> O King of night and day?
> More safe am I within thy hand,
> Than if a host did round me stand.

BREASTPLATE PRAYING

The point of breastplate praying is not that you should remain safe for the sake of any selfish pursuit of health or pleasure. Your life belongs to God and as long as you are both well and safe, you can serve him who is the center of your life's full affection. So these exercises are set up to remind you that the longer you live the fuller your service can be. Below is the simple outline of a trinitarian lorica (breastplate). In each case, celebrate the Scripture that appears and then add your own prayer phrase, invoking God's protection.

> Lord of mine, now and forever,
> to me you are one and indivisible.
> Creator God, redeemer Christ and indwelling Spirit,
> you are indestructible and eternal;
> I am weak and subject to pain and dying.

> I would serve you upon this footstool called the planet;
> it is my only possible home,
> the Roman stage where your incarnation came

to demonstrate the furthest victory that flesh can know.

I love the world you made.
It is the porch of heaven,
and there is such need here that I would serve you, Christ the Son,
till all who live without hope stumble onto Calvary
and come to know why they were born.

But to help you in reclaiming this lost world,
I must beg you to lengthen my days
and guarantee my fragile life
so I shall have all the time I need to bring
the world to your feet.

Therefore, I pray you, guard my mind so I may

Therefore I pray you, make my heart to beat for years—for I must yet serve you by

Protect me from an impure conscience, for only purity of heart can

Guard my steps, for waywardness prevents

Build in me an open interest and empathy for all those I meet who swelter in their grudges, for only those who are free of anger can

Give me full health so I may

Lord, even as Patrick hoped, may this be my prayer:

Set me on the rampart,
Give me health enough to complete the dream of God.
Amen, Father, maker of my body.
Amen, Christ, incarnate power of health and life.
Amen, Spirit, teacher of my ministry.

Amen.

I can no longer shape my lips to speak his name . . .

of all my torments that's the most fiendish.

"THE CONFESSION OF JUDAS,"
FROM *BRENDAN* BY FREDERICK BUECHNER

Then the Lord made me aware of my unbelief, so that—however late—I might recollect my offenses and turn with all my heart to the Lord my God. It was he who took heed of my insignificance. Who pitied my youth and ignorance, Who watched over me before I knew him and before I came to understand the difference between good and evil, and who protected me and comforted me as a father would his son.

PATRICK, *CONFESSIO*

6

CONFESSIONAL PRAYER

Living in Agreement with God

Prayer is a privilege that grows out of our love affair with God. Patrick's *Confession* begins with these brief but honest words, "I am Patrick, a sinner." Such a humble and open acknowledgment cleanses our life and fixes our focus on the Savior. Christ heals us even as we are in the process of confessing. Confession is but the admission of our helplessness—our need—and the subsequent redemption we find by living with Christ.

Through Christ that which we confess beckons the healing of God. But our healing comes only as we openly relate our heart-cry of sin and desire for redemption. I emphasize the word *openly*. When we acknowledge our need to be forgiven by Christ we are ushered into God's grace, and his forgiveness is ours. But our confession not only gives us a right standing with God, it equips us with spiritual power. Once again, our penitent spirits soar. All barriers between us and God are down. Our broken souls speak openly of God's grace, and his grace becomes the forte of faith.

Confession is a cry for Christ's lordship in our cleansed lives. It was inevitable in our secular age that the word *confession* would slowly fade from existence. The concept of sin began to wane during the Enlightenment and all but disappeared in the 1960s. Many psychologists began to jettison confession as the expiation of unrighteousness or aberrant behavior. They did so on the basis that sin produced guilt, and guilt was self-negating or at least self-deprecating. Just beyond the middle of the twentieth century, Karl Menninger lamented this development in his monumental *Whatever Became of Sin?* His book awoke a napping society to rise up on an elbow and take a look at its decadence. But if we felt guilty over the loss of sin, it lasted only a little while. Soon even Menninger's book receded into secondhand bookstores shelves, and the doctrine of sin was swallowed up in the smugness of pop culture. Churches still used the word *sin* and sometimes sermons were preached on it. But under the constant pressure of secularization, the word—even for the most fiery of Christians—seemed to lose its force. At the dawn of the twenty-first century *sin* seems to have lost all theological force. Unfortunately, with sin's demise, we find that there is no place for confession. Why confess when we've done nothing wrong?

We have much to learn about sin and confession from the Celts. Here, for example, is a cry for cleansing by a ninth-century Welsh poet:

> Grant me tears, O Lord, to blot out my sins;
> may I not cease from tears, O God, until I have been
>   purified.

May my heart be burned by the fire of redemption. . . .
Grant me contrition of heart so that I may not be in
   disgrace:
O Lord, protect me and grant me tears.
For the dalliance I had with women . . . grant me tears,
O Creator flowing in streams from my eyes.
For my anger, my jealousy, and my pride, a foolish deed,
   in pools
from my inmost parts bring forth tears.
My falsehood, my lying and my greed, grievous the three,
to banish them all from me . . . grant me tears.

The Celts took sin seriously because they took God seriously.
The self-sufficient, on the other hand, see God as a mere topic
of discussion. Therefore, only the needy really have a God. To
believe in God is to see yourself as both sinful and needy. Why
is this so important? For this reason: the needy confess.

WHAT IS CONFESSION?

The word *confession* has at least three meanings. First, to confess
can mean that a person openly assents to a proposition or creed.
The great Christian creeds, or confessions of faith, teach a certain body of truth (for instance, on the Trinity, the death and
resurrection of Christ, and the importance of the church). Second, to confess means that a person admits his or her guilt for
some wrong thought or act. Throughout Christian history this
has been a key understanding of the word *confession*. Third,
spiritual autobiographies, such as those of Augustine or Patrick,
are referred to as "confessions." Tying these three strands together, confession, in a Christian context, is agreeing with God

about something—either about the teachings of the church (a creed) or about our own sinfulness (our guilt). And sometimes Christians have written autobiographies that lay bare their struggles of sin and redemption, their beliefs and their lives in Christ. Thus, the third form of confession includes the other two. This is true of Patrick's *Confession*.

Here and throughout this chapter, I will be dipping into the *Confession* of Patrick—the patron saint of Ireland—to find examples of how we should view sin and confession. In other words, from Patrick's spiritual journey, I want to find evidences of how confession can free us from sin's lasting jurisdiction in our lives and unite us to Christ.

PATRICK'S *CONFESSION*

Patrick's life was unique in two ways. First, like most of the great saints and martyrs, Patrick diligently pursued union with Christ. Most of the saints, however, sought their union through cloistered prayer. Not Patrick. His hunger for God did not move him to a lonely cell of contemplation. It rather propelled him into a life of passionate political involvement. He was, for example, always speaking against the slave trade and unkind and cruel leaders (see his *Letter to Coroticus*). But his passion for justice did not run counter to his desire for a close walk with Christ, which he pursued in earnest. Second, Patrick passionately desired to see Ireland converted to Christ.

As much as Patrick wanted to live the Christ-life and enjoy Jesus in his personal devotion, he could see that the Christian life, however purely it was lived, had to be lived "in the world" (John 17:16-17). He cherished the grace that had given him union with Christ, but he knew it is not enough just to be one with Christ.

Being forgiven personally begs the question, Who else needs for-giveness? Patrick so loved being loved by God that he couldn't imagine keeping this love to himself. God was in love with the world, and all Patrick had received he knew he must pass on: "Truly, I am greatly in God's debt." he said, "He has given me great grace, that through me many people might be reborn."

Patrick believed he would take up where the apostle Paul left off. Paul had been the first to "preach to the nations"; Patrick believed he would be the last. Once his preaching had reached his international goals, he believed Jesus would come again.

> Patrick saw himself not only as a key figure in the apos-tolic task begun by the Spirit, but as the final witness whose work—as soon as he could bring it near comple-tion—would usher in the return of Christ. For most of us today, if we heard of someone with a belief that he or she had been given such a task by God we would be both skeptical and affronted by their arrogance. . . .
>
> However, such criticisms of Patrick would be wholly misplaced: his sense of his task was not that of a psycho-logically disturbed person, but a simple deduction from the facts of history and geography known to him. The gos-pel's task would be finished with the nation at the ends of the earth—now it was happening.

It is the sacred duty of all who live the confessional life to obey God. Patrick—to be obedient—had to preach Christ for he believed he was living in the final moments of history.

What's so significant is Patrick's obedience to God's call on his life. In confession he lived in agreement with God's assessment of himself and the world.

We too are called. And through confession we are released from bondage (union) to sin to take up a glad new bondage (union) of obedience to Christ. But we don't quail before our Master. We gladly accept the work; we enter the Master's fields knowing that he shares the yoke he has lain upon our shoulders. In our bondage to him—a lovely union—we learn to live daily with a confessional spirit. And it's a spirit of openness and of redemption. The prayer of confession—getting our story out—opens us up for a shadowless life with God.

AGREEING WITH GOD

Patrick's *Confession* was a literary expression that found its roots in a very simple New Testament word, *homologeo*. "If we claim to be without sin, we deceive ourselves and the truth is not in us. If we *confess* our sins, he is faithful and just and will forgive us our sins and purify us from all unrighteousness" (1 John 1:8-9, emphasis added).

Confession, as found in this wonderful Greek word, means that we are living in agreement with God. It doesn't mean so much that we are informing God of our sins as it is agreeing with him that we are sinful. Reaching this critical agreement is the beginning of personal power in prayer. Confession isn't exposing some secret part of our lives as though God is ignorant of our dark side. God knows all and certainly knows all our sins. Instead, confession is that bold step by which we stand with God, look at our dark side and agree with all that he has said about it in his Word. As simple as it sounds, this agreement with God is rare—it's hard to find. We, sadly, are all too much like Adam and Eve, crouching in the dark glen of Eden, hiding the half-eaten fruit.

Adam and Eve's era of open communion with God was short lived. Eden never seems to last long. In the Irish apocrypha the *Creation of Adam* says: "Adam was created in the third hour, was without sin for seven hours, and was driven from paradise in the tenth hour." While the actual time it took our first parents to sin is not known, for us it's usually a matter of minutes between our transgressions. We rarely put temptation at a distance—we stay too close to the tree of the knowledge of good and evil. The path behind us is strewn with the cast-off apple cores of our indulgence.

Confession then is our only hope. Confession is the bold step of putting the apple down, looking at it with God and agreeing that the fruit has our teeth marks on it. This, though, is not easy to do. Who among us likes to stand before the King of righteousness and admit both our error and our need?

When Patrick wrote his confession, he opened it with the free admission of both his sin and his need. His confession begins: "I am Patrick. I am a sinner; the most unsophisticated of people; the least among all the Christians; and to many, the most contemptible." And when it was time to stand with God and look at his life, he was quite aware that the process would be painful but good:

> And there the Lord "opened my understanding to my unbelief," so that, however late, I might become conscious of my failings. Then remembering my need, I might "turn with all my heart to the Lord my God." For it was he who had mercy on the ignorance of my youth, and who looked after me before I knew him and before I had gained wisdom or could distinguish between good and evil. Indeed, as a father consoles his son, so he protected me.

In his confession Patrick is determined to not live a single day without agreeing with God about his own sin and his need for God's grace.

By grace, our confession brings us into concord with God. And the next step after concord is union with Christ. While this term—*union*—seems not to have been familiar to Patrick, he craved, as do all good followers of Christ, the oneness that is found with God through the Spirit (Philippians 2:1; Colossians 2:2). Since Adam first sinned, humans have been separated from God. We instinctively know something is missing from our lives. There is a wall between God's holiness and sinful human nature. Only divine love can enable us to approach this barrier and dare to cross it. The Latin word for "threshold" is *limen,* and all great lovers of God look across this threshold and longing for the oneness that it forbids. But we are helpless to cross it on our own.

Here is where the eternal God in Christ drops his huge hand over the threshold of our sinfulness to hold hands with us. This is precisely what the incarnation was about. We want to be one with Christ, and this oneness is born in our willingness to live in agreement concerning our sin and his forgiveness.

D. Gwenallt Jones, one of the boldest of the Welsh poets, seemed to sense the mystical hunger of Patrick when he spoke of eradicating that barrier between sinful humanity and the holy God. He believed that in the resurrection of the body humans would be restored to union with God: "Taking to itself the body, its nostrils, sight and hearing, / To make sensuous the glories of God." This is where the prayer of confession leads! All of us, including our bodies, is brought into the glorious presence of God!

Like the apostle Paul, the ultimate agreement that Patrick

sought came with his identification with Christ's crucifixion (Galatians 2:20), which led him to "the fellowship of sharing in [Christ's] suffering" (Philippians 3:10) and thus erased that *limen* so that both he and Christ were united. D. Gwennalt Jones, in the spirit of Celtic faith, put it this way:

> Hands like these hands
> Were hammered to the Tree;
> Feet like our feet
> Were pierced: a head like our head
> Bore the mocking thorns.
> Such was the honour, the rejoicing, O Flesh
> In providing a body for the Son of God;
> The body of a Jew in Bethlehem,
> The mortal body of humankind:
> The body which was transformed in the grave
> Into a living catholic Body.

The Christian discovers a continual thirst for God that will not be quenched apart from full fellowship with God. That's the driving force behind one of the oldest Celtic hymns, "Be Thou My Vision."

> Be Thou my Vision, O Lord of my heart;
> Naught is all else to me, save that Thou art,
> Thou my best thought, by day and by night,
> Waking or sleeping, Thy presence my light.
>
> Be Thou my Wisdom, Thou my true Word,
> I ever with Thee, Thou with me Lord.
> Thou my great Father, I thy dear son
> Thou in me dwelling, I with Thee one.

"I with Thee one" clearly reflects the hunger for union behind the prayer of confession.

NAKEDNESS AND UNION WITH CHRIST

The ultimate goal of confession is unity with Christ. How do we achieve unity with Christ in practical terms? Perhaps the metaphor of naked lovers best expresses the unity we seek. Genesis 2:25 helps us understand: "The man and his wife were both naked and they felt no shame." The point of this passage is that there is nothing, absolutely nothing, coming between the fellowship that Adam and Eve experienced. They have nothing to hide from each other or from God.

Nakedness is a powerful metaphor of acceptance. And a kind of nakedness is required for spiritual intimacy to reach its zenith. No marriage is healthy when the couple cannot be joyfully naked and yet feel no shame in each other's embrace. When anything stands between lovers and their embrace, true intimacy is lost.

Union with Christ entails utter openness between the believer and Christ. Intimacy is born when all our sins are confessed, and we come just as we are into the presence of God. There, stripped of our pride and self-will, we are fully in his presence. Then we, like Adam and Eve before the Fall, walk with God. Nothing is hidden. All is openly declared. Nothing questionable casts its shadow on our relationship.

This same concept arises in Franco Zeffirelli's 1972 movie *Brother Sun, Sister Moon*. When Francis (1181-1226) finally confessed Christ after being intimidated by the courts, he dropped his royal robes, declared "I am born again!" and walked off naked into the fields. The next time he appeared in the film he was dressed in sackcloth, crude and rustic. The coarse cloth of a field monk is in effect a kind of nakedness. For it wraps the body in humility and all traces of arrogance are gone.

Now we must come into the presence of a holy God and, like Francis of Assisi, take off our clothing of guilt and confusion. After we have thrown off these soiled coverings, we must stand with God and agree that we have been unfaithful and that we have nothing to offer to God. We must confess with Isaiah that "all our righteous acts are like filthy rags" (Isaiah 64:6). No wonder Meilyr Son of Gwalchmai wrote during the Middle Ages

> May God grant me, may I be granted mercy,
> May no evil lack defeat me,
> May being righteous on account of my gift cleanse me
> And the world, which I know well, be shaken.
> May I deserve God's favor, the Lord glorify me,
> And give me entrance to the home of heaven.

Much earlier in time, realizing his own desperate situation and his inability to overcome sin on his own, the apostle Paul confesses: "I know that nothing good lives in me, that is, in my sinful nature. For I have the desire to do what is good, but I cannot carry it out. . . . What a wretched man that I am! Who will rescue me from the body of this death?" (Romans 7:18, 24). Such sweet peace ever comes from being reconciled with God. An anonymous, early Irish cry for cleansing put it this way:

> Jesus, forgive my sins.
> Forgive the sins that I can remember, and also the sins I
>   have forgotten.
> Forgive the wrong actions I have committed, and the right
>   actions I have omitted.

> Forgive the times I have been weak in the face of temptation, and those when I have been stubborn in the face of correction.
>
> Forgive the times I have been proud of my own achievements, and those when I have failed to boast of your works.
>
> Forgive the harsh judgments I have made of others, and the leniency I have shown to myself.
>
> Forgive the lies I have told to others, and the truths I have avoided.
>
> Forgive me of the pain I have caused others, and the indulgence I have shown to myself.
>
> Jesus have pity on me, and make me whole.

John Newton wrote the lament for us all: "Amazing grace, how sweet the sound that saved a wretch like me."

We must confess our wretchedness. We are hiding out in Eden with the fruit—half-eaten—still in our hand, and we have been discovered. We look down in shame and suddenly realize that we are exposed, with no place to run and no place to hide. We are, to say the least, wretched. There is no justification for our state. What do we do? It's too late for paltry excuses. We cannot pass the buck. But as hard as it is, we must confess our willful disobedience to the holy and righteous God.

We must be willing to stand with God and look at ourselves, agree with him that we are naked, and seek the wholeness that prefaces our first step toward union with Christ. In short, when we confess we say, "Lord, this is me, and here's what I've done." We confess as Patrick did: "Here I am . . . a sinner." Sedulus Scottus cried as Patrick cried—in a day far separate from our own.

I read and write and teach, philosophy peruse.
I eat and freely drink, with rhymes invoke the muse,
I call on heaven's throne both night and day,
Snoring I sleep, and stay awake and pray.
And sin and fault inform each act I plan.
Ah! Christ . . . pity this miserable man.

We can never achieve union with God by clinging to our self-sufficiency. Recognizing and admitting our need in confession creates a heart cry for oneness.

CONFESSION: THE END OF OUR UNSETTLED LONGINGS

Confession brings us to a new dimension of living. It gives us the ability to escape all false opinions of ourselves. We who confess are driven by the haunting question, What's wrong with me? There is a gut-level, unsettled feeling that things are not right with us or the world. We want things to be settled.

The initial step in confession is recognizing that all's not right with us. So we search for an answer, not knowing where the search will lead. Regarding the approach-avoidance dilemma of those who search, Francis Thompson in "The Hound of Heaven" describes how we flee from God down the corridors of our hearts and minds. We hide from him under running laughter. We want him, even as we fear him. We represent the most noble of neuroses of fearing and craving God at the same time. Our fear makes us tentative when we approach him. Our cravings drive us forward to locate him and merge with him in spiritual union.

The Germans call this unsettled state *sensucht,* homesickness. What Patrick sought was an end to his homesickness; he needed divine stability. For without God there are no pilgrimages of consequence. Esther de Waal put it this way:

> The Welsh saint of the fifth century, St. Brynach, who had his church at Nevern in Pembrokeshire, in speaking of home adds one vital word to my understanding of the journey of the *peregrini:* the need to find a home, to be at home in all the many levels that that word can carry. For to be earthed and grounded in the reality of being at home in one's self and in the world around touches on something that is essential, necessary, if my being is to have a form and shape.

We are not at home till we fully agree with God and find union with him. Augustine freely confessed, "Our heart is restless until it rests in you." For all the saints, the only legitimate, final definition is union with Christ. Anything less is but a step in the journey, never the destination.

A THREE-STEP PILGRIMAGE

Confession, whether formal (like Patrick's) or informal (private prayers), always entails a three-step pilgrimage.

1. A desperate longing for God. Augustine's own confession was driven by fear and longing for something more. He was desperate to find the one thing that filled his longing—union with God. In his *Confession* he gives a summary of his search:

> I asked the earth and it answered "I am not he." . . . I asked the sea and its creatures, and they answered: "We are not your God, seek higher!" I asked the whole air and every-

thing in it, and it answered: "Anaximenes was wrong—I am not your God." I asked the heavens, the sun, moon, and stars and they answered: "Neither are we God whom you seek." . . . I asked the whole frame of the universe about my God and it answered me: "I am not he, but he made me."

The Celts like Augustine were seeking relief from their huge need to be forgiven, to be justified, to be united with that perfect Reason that is beyond all reason. Only when they reached that stage could they take step two, the call to serve the Giver of reason.

2. *Agreeing with God that our sin is sin.* This step cannot seem to be very complicated, for it seems the most straightforward of definitions. And yet when caught any where near the threshold of shame, we suddenly feel the bite of ostracism and begin some attempt to justify whatever sin we have been caught at. We work hard with the most outlandish self-defenses to make ourselves look lily white when we are grimy with evidence to the contrary.

The Celts have for their witness the confession of St. Patrick. Within the first five words of his confession he manages to say the "s" word—he openly confesses his sin. But Patrick's upfront honesty is not the usual way we deal with sin. Our tendency is to hide from the pain of open confession—dodging openness on the subject of sin began in Eden. When Adam was actually discovered with the forbidden fruit, obviously gnawed upon, he basically said to God, "It was the woman you gave me that is really guilty." And Eve says, in effect, "I wouldn't have done this except the serpent beguiled me." Here in the first instance of first sin; nobody steps up to the plate and says "I sinned."

Adam and Eve's response was passed on to the human race. The phrase in politics is called the "cover up." And it is generally thought by those who cover political events for the press that "cover up" is a kind of sin that is generally worse than the sin it "covers up." In one of the greatest political scandals I can remember, the entire presidential Cabinet became addicted to covering up a national crime. And finally when the web of lies had become too burdensome to carry or extend any further, one of the Cabinet members laid down the apple of excuse-making and said, "I did it, they did it, we all did it." The president's resignation from office was immediate, but sooner or later the coming clean let the nation begin to heal.

It is said that when George Washington was asked if he really cut down the cherry tree, he began his confession with "I cannot tell a lie." The story is likely a fable, but it is a pleasant one. If Adam had started out by saying "I cannot tell a lie" and could have passed down *that* tendency to the human race instead of the legacy of rationalization, just think how much better off the world would be?

Patrick of Ireland understood that, as simple as it is, the best way to begin a confession was to say up front, "I, Patrick, a sinner . . ." Everything after such a beginning is open and honest and completes the beginning of the second step in the pilgrimage of confession.

3. Serving God in the world. It is the oddest of paradoxes that in giving ourselves away we find ourselves. Yet this self-regard is not really selfish. Those who belong to Christ do not have their own agenda. Those who are one with the Savior find their strength not in their own agenda but in that of the Savior.

Is such an agenda of ministry bondage? No. His burden is liberty, his yoke is light. Rhys Prydderch wrote: "It is better to be in prison with Christ than to be free without him. . . . Many of God's saints were killed, but not one of them was ever conquered."

It is only when our confession agrees to ultimate service that we find, the most rigorous yet most joyous service. We come to be like Christ who did not shrink from his most arduous service: human redemption. We, who take up our crosses to die with him, come to know the fellowship of suffering (Philippians 3:10). In agreeing to the bondage of obedience, we are free. Christ's finest ministry to us was Calvary. So is ours to him. In Matthew 16, Peter confesses Christ and within the next few years, both of them are martyrs. But are they in bondage? Certainly not. Pennar Davies wrote of the liberty owned by the crucified one.

> Christ is the Free Man. Look at him, my soul, at his nakedness, his blood, his sweat. The Eternal Prisoner! The soldiers beat him, cursing and laughing drunkenly. They feel that they represent a higher civilization than his, a richer culture and an infinitely better race. In each blow there is contempt and greed. Are not the Roman soldiers masters of the world?
>
> Even in his anguish and shame Christ takes pity on the soldiers in their captivity.
>
> He is the Free Man. Gaze on him, my soul. Does he have wealth, worldly power, an influential position in the organization of the country? No. He has nothing but a body now and the soldiers treat that body as they please. Flesh, blood, skin, bones, hair—he has only these things

now, and the kingdom of Hell wants to take these things from him.

Look at him my soul. He is a Free Man; the only free man in Jerusalem.

Pilate's empire is a prison; Caiaphas' religion is a prison; Judas' dream is a prison; Peter's confusion is a prison; Herod's ambition is a prison; having been freed from his cell Barabbas' rebellious movement is a prison. Christ alone is free.

My soul stands with him. There, by his side, under the lash of soldiers, freedom is to be found.

Christ's cross was the Father's agenda for both his son and us. Our cross is Jesus' agenda for us in the world. Agreeing to it by confession, we find our place of ministry in the world.

THE MARRIAGE OF THE FORGIVER AND THE FORGIVEN

But it is not just our ministry we agree to in confession. We experience our belonging to Christ through confession. When we agree with God, his grace and our need become blurred in his ownership of our lives, in our union with him. His sinlessness destroys our sinfulness; his grace overcomes our need; and in union with him our failures are covered by his victory.

Union with Christ is the hunger of all saints. Certainly it is true of Patrick. He could never get over the notion that though he was unlovely and unworthy of grace, God had rescued him. Through his *Confession*, Patrick made plain his dependence on God.

But I know one thing without any doubt and with the greatest assurance: . . . I was like a stone lying in the deepest mire, and the "he who is mighty" came and in his mercy, raised me up. He most truly raised me on high and set me on a rampart. So I ought to cry out with all my strength and render thanks to the Lord, for his blessings are indeed great, here and in eternity, and beyond all that the human mind can imagine.

From the beginning of his journey into union with Christ, he was always under the attack of Satan. He describes being tempted by Satan in one instance as feeling like he had an "enormous rock" on him, saying, "I lost all power over my limbs." He then saw the sun rising and called out, *"Helia, Helia!"* And then "the sun's splendor fell on me and dispelled immediately all the heaviness from me and I believe that Christ, my Lord assisted me and his spirit had already cried out through me." The name of the Druid sun god was *Helios.* From the context it seems that Patrick was really calling on an old pagan deity. He was too new in the faith to really understand everything he needed to know about calling on God. But the real key to understanding was that he saw the Spirit of God as an Intercessor whose constant intercession had saved him from the attack of Satan.

Near the end of the confession, Patrick admits and even celebrates that *we* is the grand pronoun that we shall wear when we are joined with Christ in eternity. Our future life will not be solo, for we will have merged with Christ once and for all. Then the result of our prayers will be achieved. We shall indeed be one.

And, if at any time I have "imitated something that is good" for the sake of my God whom I love, then I ask him to grant me that I may shed my blood "for his name's sake" with those proselytes and captives, even if this means that I should lack even a tomb, or that my corpse be horribly chopped up by dogs and wild beasts, or that the "birds of heaven devour it." I do hereby declare that should this happen to me, that I should have gained my soul as well as my body. For should any of these things happen, there is no doubt that on the day we shall arise in the brightness of the sun, this is in the glory of Christ Jesus our redeemer, we shall be "sons of the living God" and "fellow heirs with Christ" and "conformed to his image"; "for from him and through him and in him" we shall reign.

Confession brings us close to God, but this closeness can be very dangerous.

This was not the rather clinical rationalistic ethos of much of today's religion, but rather a colourful expression of the relations of the divine with the human, dangerous but very exciting. Even the great Colm Cille had to watch his step. According to tradition a friendly angel visited him regularly.

But one day St. Colm Cille must have said something out of the way for the angel hit him a slap across the face which left its mark on him for life. This teeming world of supernaturals must have made the doctrine of the Communion of Saints particularly dear and accessible to the Irish.

The confessional life is one that must be lived very close—dangerously close—to God. It is said that when Brendan met Brigit, after Brendan had encountered a nearly fatal meeting with a great whale at sea, the following conversation occurred:

"Tell me," says St. Brigit, "is your mind constantly on God, are you constantly aware of him?" "Well," says St. Brendan, "I am generally aware of God, but I live a very busy and dangerous life. Often the sea is very rough and storms arise and on these occasions I forget all about God as I am so preoccupied trying to keep afloat."

"That is the explanation," says Brigit, "for since the first day I set my mind on God I have never taken it away from him and I never will."

Anyone who takes up the truly confessional life will live dangerously close to God. There the confession caught up in the wonder and fear of the confessional life would live to confess with F. W. Faber:

They love thee, little, if at all,
Who do not fear thee much
If love is thine attraction, Lord!
Fear is thy very touch.

And so we are called to live the confessional life and called to a glorious life of dying and living in fear and wonder.

CONFESSION

The confession, whether written or prayed spontaneously, generally majors on these three things: a desperate longing for God; agreeing with God that our sin is sin; and serving God in the world.

Confession is the prayer that is hardest to formalize. When the form remains flexible and unplanned, the confessor can achieve that atmosphere of openness that keeps us real. So the point is not to address it too artistically, so that we are composing a thing of beauty but to approach it with utter honesty so that we too are real. Confession may seem like an art form when we read the confessions of Augustine or Patrick, but in reality the issue of coming clean before God must be an issue of on-the-spot integrity. Still, these glorious literary confessions can serve as articles of worship, and more than that, they can serve as models of content as to what we ought to say. So to begin with, you might want to pray the Scripture, as found in Psalm 51. Then you might want to phrase your own confession, using the three issues of confession as listed above. Pray the following prayer and then compose your own statements of longing, admission and service.

> I come to you Father, acknowledging my longing after you.
> I come to you Son of the Father, acknowledging that my sin has met the cross.
> I come to you Spirit, asking you to fill me so that I may keep my place of ministry in bringing the world to a full confession of its own.
> To you, merciful Father, I pray,
> against you have I sinned and done what is evil in your sight.
> To you, merciful Son of the Father, I pray,
> wash away all my iniquity and cleanse me from my sin.
> To you, merciful Spirit, I pray,
> create in me a pure heart.

Now believing in your cleansing and trusting in your mercy, I offer you this confession:

I, _____, *freely acknowledge my sin.*
I take no credit for my redemption,
yet I know it stands in place forever, as eternal as grace itself.
Give ear to my desperate longing for you, O Father.

For this is how I feel my neediness, and express my longing:

I agree with you that I have sinned. I express what my sins have cost
you and how in the past they have barred me from the fullest rela-
tionship I might have had with you.

I am seeking that perfect expression of your will for me in the world.
Help me discover what every moment holds for me so that I can serve
you in the exact manner you will equip me to serve. Here is the sub-
stance of my search:

Here is the story of how I first met you, how I first felt a longing for
your love.

Here I rehearse my first feeling of brokenness for our years of separation and the joy of my homecoming.

As a final expression of my confession, I write out here in prayer my calling in the world. As far as I know here is what you have called me to do and when my service is to begin.

Father to you I give thanks for my purpose.
Son to you I give thanks for your cross and my redemption.
Spirit to you I give thanks for empowering my ministry in the world.

Amen, Father Almighty.
Amen, Son who saves.
Amen, Spirit who empowers.

AFTERWORD

The Celts had a way of seeing God that fed off a passion that crystallized in what the Welsh called *gorfoleddu,* "ecstatic rejoicing." The word is more than praise, and it is certainly more than prayer. In fact, it is a kind of compulsion that caused the worshiper to seek Christ with utter abandon, which was driven by a mind frame of zealous worship.

Diarmuid O'Laoghaire wrote of this warm force in "The Celtic Monk at Prayer":

Lord, be it thine,
Unfaltering praise of mine!
To Thee my whole heart's love be given
Of earth and heaven Thou King divine!

Lord, be it thine,
Unfaltering praise of mine!
And, O Pure Prince! make clear my way
To serve and pray at thy sole shrine!

Lord, be it thine,
Unfaltering praise of mine!

O Father of souls that long,
Take this my song and make it thine!

It is *gorfoleddu* that prompts our need to pray, and it is its ab-
sence that causes us not to pray. This is similar to the *neart,* except that the *neart,* which springs out of all the things that God
has created, brings the external force of his power into our personal lives. The *gorfolledu,* on the other hand, springs spontaneously out of our personal lives and reaches toward God with the
exuberance of praise. These are rather two sides of the same
coin. The *neart* is the force of the reaching God, and the *gorfoleddu* is the eager spirit of the reaching worshiper. Where
these two passions meet real prayer—yes, even authentic
faith—comes to be.

Most evangelicals I know want to achieve power in prayer, but
they speak of this power as though it is totally God-conferred
(*neart* as it were). What is often lacking in their prayer life is a
genuine passion that wants to be with God for the sake of union
with Christ (the *gorfoleddu* of their own eager spirits).

Those who speak of achieving "power in prayer" are generally seeking it for petition and intercession. Those most eager to
talk to God for the sheer pleasure of being in his presence are
serving their inner exuberance of loving God for no end in
mind except the joy of being in his presence. Genuine prayer
rarely emanates from how-to sources. It is always born from the
hunger and the passion that rises from the believer's hunger for
a relationship with the Almighty.

Hopefully our trek together has caused you to pray in a new
way. But above all, I hope that this journey has helped you to
see in a new way. I hope the Celts have at least reminded us that

these six prayer windows that open on the reality of the God's transcendent realm are not so much procedures on how to pray as they are the facets of a new understanding of prayer—a new worldview.

Why can such a worldview enliven and enrich your life in Christ? Because it has the power to excite within you a nobler understanding of the nature of talking *with* God. (Notice I did not say talking *to* God.) Prayer, at best, is a conversation of lovers, and when either side starts only talking *to* and quits talking *with* all real conversation is over. But the conversation is the point. Those who only talk to God to talk him into things have generally made God their lackey who is constantly subject to their feelings of need and want. Those who seek him for the joy of being in his presence have been motivated by a passion for his presence. When this becomes the hallmark of our devotion, then our lives are spent as a kind of rehearsal for heaven.

But if, throughout our lives, we have only gone to God in prayer asking him for "stuff," we shall find ourselves very quiet, not knowing what to say when our asking season is over. This *gorfoleddu,* this ecstatic rejoicing speaks of the uncontrollable joy of being in his presence. It is a word that speaks of the high romance of prayer. Those who come to know it, realize that it's a word that is too delirious with love ever to measure its propriety. It is like lovers separated by war and distance, when they approach the time of reunion, are not to be held accountable for wild joy. In such moments, the lovers have no lists of needs they wish supplied. The moment is the gift. Togetherness is the prize of life.

NOTES

To the Reader

pp. 8-10   From my limited studies of the Celts: The reality behind much of the present study of the Celtic Church and Celtic spirituality is in dispute. It is very difficult to separate legend from history. To get a better handle on this, I recommend Ted Olsen's *Christianity and the Celts* (Downers Grove, Ill.: InterVarsity Press, 2003), and Ian Bradley, *Celtic Christianity: Making Myths and Chasing Dreams* (New York: St. Martin's Press, 1999).

p. 9   "The remains of this once great civilization": Seán Ó Duinn, *Where Three Streams Meet* (Dublin: Columba Press, 2000), p. 21.

p. 11   "Father, all powerful and ever-living God": Thomas O'Loughlin, *Journeys on the Edges* (New York: Orbis, 2000), pp. 69-70.

Introduction

p. 16   "The Celt was very much a God-intoxicated man": Seán Ó Duinn, *Where Three Streams Meet* (Dublin: Columba Press, 2000), p. 9.

p. 16   "While later Christians in the Celtic lands": Thomas O'Loughlin, *Journeys on the Edges* (New York: Orbis, 2000), pp. 58-59.

p. 18   "When little is demanded from members, little is given": Ian

Smith, quoted in Ian Bradley, *Celtic Christian Communities* (Kelowna, Canada: Northstone Publishing, 2000), p. 56.

p. 20   Patrick and Columba were pastors: T. Head, quoted in Bradley, *Celtic Christian Communities,* p. 166.

p. 20   "Thou King of the Moon": "Rune of the Muthairn," in Alexander Carmichael, *Carmina Gadelica* (New York: Lindisfarne Press, 1992), p. 43.

p. 21   "Behold the Lightener of the Stars": "The Lightener of the Stars," in Carmichael, *Carmina Gadelica,* p. 46.

p. 21   "In St. Patrick's Breastplate": Ó Duinn, *Where Three Streams Meet,* p. 84.

p. 22   "I am bending my knee": "A Prayer for Grace," in Carmichael, *Carmina Gadelica,* p. 44.

p. 22   Trinitarian prayer ending with "Will gently place it hither on my tongue": "Charm for the Eye" in Carmichael, *Carmina Gadelica,* p. 409.

p. 23   Celts praying against slurs of speech: "Charm Against Venom," in Carmichael, *Carmina Gadelica,* p. 206.

p. 23   Trinitarian prayer ending with "Three just and holy": (NA) in Carmichael, *Carmina Gadelica,* p. 383.

p. 26   "The Celtic image of pilgrimage": Hugh Connolly, quoted in Bradley, *Celtic Christian Communities,* p. 209.

p. 26   They were missionaries who went abroad: O'Loughlin, *Journeys on the Edges,* p. 82.

p. 26   "Blest be the boat!": From "The Sea Prayer," in Carmichael, *Carmina Gadelica,* p. 123.

p. 27   "God, omit not this woman": "Death Blessing," in Carmichael, *Carmina Gadelica,* p. 67.

p. 30   "I will build up my fire today": Ó Duinn, *Where Three Streams Meet,* p. 230.

Chapter 1: Trinity Prayer

pp. 36-37   morning prayer ending with "Bestow upon us fullness in our need": "Rune Before Prayer," in Alexander Carmichael, *Carmina Gadelica* (New York: Lindisfarne Press, 1992), p. 35.

p. 37   noontide prayer ending with "Each day and night give us Thy peace": From "A Prayer for Grace," in Carmichael, *Carmina Gadelica*, p. 35.

p. 40   "I praise the threefold": "Praise to the Trinity," *The Black Book of Carmarthen*, in Oliver Davies, *Celtic Christianity in Medieval Wales: The Origin of the Welsh Spiritual Tradition* (Cardiff, 1996), pp. 28-29. *The Black Book of Carmarthen* was composed in the second half of the thirteenth century, likely in a Cistercian monastery such as Hendy-Gwyn or in the Augustinian Priory of St. John the Evangelist at Carmarthen.

p. 41   Ian Bradley says . . . no record of liturgical services: Ian Bradley, *Celtic Christian Communities* (Kelowna, Canada: Northstone Press, 2000), p. 123.

p. 41   Whether they worshiped: Ibid., pp. 130-33.

pp. 41-42   "Thou art the pure love of the clouds": *Carmina Gadelica*, in Oliver Davies and Fiona Bowie, *Celtic Christian Spirituality* (New York: Continuum, 1995), p. 136.

pp. 43-44   "The tempests howl": T. O. Fiaich, *Columbanus in His Own Words* (Dublin: Veritas, 1974), p. 112.

Chapter 2: Scripture Prayer

p. 54   "So, for instance when we meet the word field": Thomas O'Loughlin, *Journeys on the Edges* (New York: Orbis, 2000), p. 40.

p. 55   "The Scriptures stood on the edge": Ibid., pp. 40-41.

p. 56   making the Scriptures personal: Of course, we need to be very careful in modifying the Scripture. These variations presented in this chapter aren't necessary for praying the Scriptures since the Scriptures are very personal just as they are.

p. 60   "I'm pressing on the upward way": Johnson Oatman Jr., "Higher Ground" (1898).

p. 60   "O Beulah Land": Edgar P. Stites, "Beulah Land" (1876).

p. 61   "Maol Póil Ó Cinnaetha, abbot": Seán Ó Duinn, *Where*

Three Streams Meet (Dublin: Columba Press, 2000), pp. 204-5.

p. 67   "Central's never busy, always on the line": Frederick M. Lehman, "The Royal Telephone" (1919).

Chapter 3: Long, Wandering Prayer

p. 73   "Everyday you depart": Ian Bradley, *Celtic Christian Communities* (Kelowna, Canada: Northstone Publishing, 2000), p. 204.

p. 74   Barinthus told Brendan the land was full: See *The Voyage of Brendan,* in Oliver Davies, *Celtic Spirituality* (New York: Paulist Press, 1999), p. 155.

p. 74   "God is our helper": Ted Olsen, *Christianity and the Celts* (Downers Grove, Ill.: InterVarsity Press, 2003), pp. 122-23.

p. 75   "Let us praise God": *The Wisdom of the Celts,* ed. and comp. David Adam (Grand Rapids: Eerdmans, 1996), p. 21.

p. 76   "I am Judas, most wretched": Quoted in Davies, *Celtic Spirituality,* p. 184.

p. 77   "Thou shalt go no further, nor touch the man": Columba, quoted in Ted Olson, *Christianity and the Celts* (Downers Grove, Ill.: InterVarsity Press, 2003), p. 113.

p. 77   "The Celtic image of pilgrimage": Hugh Connolly, quoted in Bradley, *Celtic Christian Communities,* p. 209.

p. 78   "Whether walking, working, reading or praying, one is in two worlds": Thomas O'Loughlin, *Journeys on the Edges: The Celtic Tradition* (New York: Orbis, 2000), p. 40.

p. 80   There is a yearning to make peace: Mark McIntosh, quoted in Atherton, *Celts and Christians,* p. 114.

p. 80   "Oh the comfort, the inexpressible comfort": George Eliot, quoted in Bradley, *Celtic Christian Communities,* p. 111.

p. 82   "One day an island appeared to them in the distance": *The Voyage of Brendan,* in Davies, *Celtic Spirituality,* p. 172.

p. 82   "God, bless to me this day": "The Journey Prayer," in Alexander Carmichael, *Carmina Gadelica* (New York: Lindisfarne Press, 1992), p. 244.

p. 83   "Jesu! Only-begotten Son and Lamb": "Jesus the Encompasser," in Carmichael, *Carmina Gadelica,* pp. 212-13.

pp. 84-86   "Blest be the boat": "Sea Prayer," in Carmichael, *Carmina Gadelica,* pp. 123-24.

pp. 86-87   "I set the keeping of Christ about thee:" "The Gospel of Christ," in Carmichael, *Carmina Gadelica,* p. 248.

pp. 87-88   "To accompany other people, along with their loved ones": Penelope Wilcock, quoted in Bradley, *Celtic Christian Communities,* p. 112.

Chapter 4: Nature Prayer

p. 94   "My mother would be asking us to sing": Quoted in Seán Ó Duinn, *Where Three Streams Meet* (Dublin: Columba Press, 2000), pp. 218-19.

p. 95   "Infinite and wise is God": W. Leslie Richards, "The Creator," in *Cerddi'r Cyfnos,* trans. Cynthia and Saunders Davies (Gwynedd, U.K.: Gwasg Gee, 1986), quoted in *A Celtic Primer,* ed. Brendan O'Malley (New York: Morehouse Publishing, 2002), pp. 183-84.

p. 95   "When the true shepherd speaks": Morgan Llwyd, quoted in *A Celtic Primer,* comp. Brendan O'Malley (Harrisburg, Penn.: Morehouse, 2002), p. 183.

p. 96   "The Eucharist is a concentrate": Brendan, quoted in *A Celtic Primer,* comp. Brendan O'Malley (Harrisburg, Penn.: Morehouse, 2002), p. 207.

pp. 96-97   "I offer Thee / Every wave that ever moved": "Glorificamus Te" in *Celtic Primer,* pp. 172-73.

pp. 97-98   "You appointed the sun in heaven to begin": Geoffrey Cumming and R. C. Jasper, *Prayers of the Eucharist, Early and Reformed* (New York: Liturgical Press, 1980), quoted in Ó Duinn, *Where Three Streams Meet,* pp. 239-40.

p. 99   "The fair maid who": Iona Opie and Moira Tatem, *A Dictionary of Superstitions* (New York: Oxford University Press, 1992), p. 246.

p. 101   "Honey under ground": From *The Celtic Gift of Nature,* in

Alexander Carmichael, *Carmina Gadelica* (Edinburgh: Floris Books, 2004), p. 19.

p. 101   nature praise and God: The Celtic Christians were trinitarians, not pantheists.

pp. 101-2   "Old men in the Isles still uncover their heads": Carmichael, *Carmina Gadelica*, p. 19.

p. 102   "I love the Irish Catholic church": Colm Kilcoyne, quoted in Timothy Joyce, *Celtic Christianity* (New York: Orbis, 2001), p. 43.

p. 103   "I wish, O Son of the living God, eternal ancient King": Manchán, quoted in Ó Duinn, *Where Three Streams Meet*, p. 193.

pp. 103-4   "Let us pray to God the Father, God the Son": Moucan, in *Celtic Primer*, p. 244.

p. 105   "There is a little tup": Seán Ó Duinn, *The Rites of Brigid*, (Dublin: Columba Press, 2005), p. 223.

p. 106   "Basically, the *Plundering of Hell* is an expression": Ó Duinn, *Where Three Streams Meet*, p. 126.

p. 107   "A common theme throughout Celtic religion": Ted Olsen, *Christianity and the Celts* (Downers Grove, Ill.: InterVarsity Press, 2003), p. 70.

p. 107   "I rise today, / in the power's strength *[neart]*, invoking the Trinity": Seán Ó Duinn introduces the concept of *neart* to St. Patrick's breastplate in *Where Three Streams*, p. 84.

p. 108   "God-intoxicated people": Joyce, *Celtic Christianity*, p. 113.

pp. 108-9   "O star-like sun, O guiding light": Ibid., p. 161.

p. 109   "The beauty of summer, its days long and slow": "The Loves of Taliesin," in Oliver Davies and Fiona Bowie, *Celtic Christian Spirituality* (New York: Continuum, 1995), pp. 55-56.

p. 110   "When Christ, the most high Lord": Columba, *Altus Prosator*, in Ian Bradley, *Celtic Christian Communities* (Kelowna, Canada: Northstone, 2000), pp. 157-58.

p. 111   "Almighty Creator, it is you who have made the land": Thomas, *Almighty Creator*, in Davies and Bowie, *Celtic Christian Spirituality*, pp. 55-56.

Chapter 5: Lorica Prayer

p. 121   "a highly militaristic conception of Christian life": Seán Ó Duinn, *Where Three Streams Meet* (Dublin: Columba Press, 2000), p. 127.

p. 121   Satan "realises that Christ derives his power from God": *Études Celtiques,* in ibid., p. 131.

p. 122   "The tempests howl, the storms dismay": "The Boat Song," in David Adam, *The Wisdom of The Celts* (Grand Rapids: Eerdmans, 1996), p. 22.

p. 123   "May the way of God direct us": Patrick, "The Power of God," in Adam, *Wisdom of the Celts,* p. 17.

p. 123   "I was like a stone": Patrick, *Confessio,* in Ted Olsen, *Christianity and the Celts* (Downers Grove, Ill.: InterVarsity Press, 2003), p. 67.

p. 124   "For Christ's sake, [Alban] bore the most horrible torments": Bede, *A History of the English Church and People,* in Olsen, *Christianity and the Celts,* p. 42 (emphasis added).

pp. 125-26   "O God, defend me everywhere": "Breastplate of Laidcenn," in Oliver Davies, *Celtic Spirituality* (New York: Paulist Press, 1999), pp. 289-92.

pp. 126-27   "I rise today: / in the power of Christ's birth and baptism": "Breastplate of St. Patrick," in Davies, *Celtic Spirituality,* pp. 118-20.

p. 129   "The Three that are the oldest": Ó Duinn, *Where Three Streams Meet,* p. 163.

p. 130   "I make this bed tonight": Ibid., p. 165.

p. 131   "Alone with none but thee, my God": Irish hymn attributed to Columba, in Ian Bradley, *Celtic Christian Communities* (Kelowna, Canada: Northstone, 2000), p. 210.

Chapter 6: Confessional Prayer

pp. 136-37   "Grant me tears, O Lord, to blot out my sins": Anonymous, in *Celtic Spirituality* (New York: Paulist Press, 1999), pp. 261-62.

p. 139   "Truly, I am greatly in God's debt": Patrick, *Confessio,* in

Oliver Davies and Thomas O'Loughlin, *Celtic Spirituality* (New York: Paulist Press, 1999), p. 76.

p. 139 "Patrick saw himself not only as a key figure": Thomas O'Loughlin, *Journeys on the Edges* (New York: Orbis, 2000), p. 57.

p. 141 "Adam was created in the third hour": Quoted in Davies and O'Loughlin, *Celtic Spirituality*, p. 327.

p. 141 Adam and Eve in the Garden of Eden: The Bible does not specify what kind of fruit the tree of the knowledge of good and evil produced (see Genesis 3:2-6).

p. 141 "I am Patrick. I am a sinner": Patrick, *Confessio,* in Davies and O'Loughlin, *Celtic Spirituality,* p. 67.

p. 141 "And there the Lord 'opened my understanding'": Ibid.

p. 142 "Taking to itself the body, its nostrils": Gwenallt Jones, *Flesh and Spirit,* in *Celts and Christians,* ed. Mark Atherton (Cardiff: University of Wales Press, 2002), p. 154.

p. 143 "Hands like these hands": Ibid., p. 164

p. 143 "Be Thou my Vision": "Be Thou My Vision," attributed to Dallan Forgaill (eighth century Irish), trans. Mary E. Byrne (1905).

p. 145 "May God grant me, may I be granted mercy": Oliver Davies, ed. and trans., "Meilyr Son of Gwalchmai's Ode to God," in *Celtic Spirituality,* Classics of Western Spirituality (New York: Paulist Press, 1999), p. 279.

pp. 145-46 "Jesus, forgive my sins": Brendan O'Malley, ed., *A Celtic Primer* (New York: Morehouse Publishing, 2002), pp. 95-96.

p. 147 "I read and write and teach, philosophy peruse": Ibid., p. 96.

p. 148 "The Welsh saint of the fifth century, St. Brynach": Esther De Waal, *The Celtic Way of Prayer* (New York: Doubleday, 1997), p. 8.

p. 148 "Our heart is restless": Augustine *Confessions* 1.1.

pp. 148-49 "I asked the earth and it answered 'I am not he' ": Augustine *Confessions* 10.6.

p. 151 "It is better to be in prison with Christ": O'Malley, *Celtic Primer,* p. 182.

pp. 151-52	"Christ is the Free Man": Ibid.
p. 152	Patrick made plain his dependence on God: Davies and O'Loughlin, *Celtic Spirituality,* p. 29.
pp. 152-53	"But I know one thing without any doubt": Patrick, *Confessio,* in Davies and O'Loughlin, *Celtic Spirituality,* p. 70.
p. 153	"The sun's splendor": Ibid., p. 73.
pp. 153-54	"And, if at any time I have 'imitated something that is good'": Patrick, *Confessio,* in Davies and O'Loughlin, *Celtic Spirituality,* p. 82.
p. 154	"This was not the rather clinical rationalistic ethos": Seán Ó Duinn, *Where Three Streams Meet* (Dublin: Columba Press, 2000), p. 76.
p. 154	" 'Tell me,' says St. Brigit": Ibid., p. 88.
p. 155	"They love thee, little, if at all": Frederick William Faber, "The Fear of the Lord," in A. W. Tozer, *The Christian Book of Mystical Verse* (Harrisburg, Penn.: Christian Publications, 1991), p. 19.

Afterword

| pp. 159-60 | "Lord, be it thine": Diarmuid O'Laoghaire, "The Celtic Monk at Prayer," *Monastic Studies* 14 (1983): 133, quoted in Esther de Waal, *The Celtic Way of Prayer* (New York: Doubleday, 1997), p. 188. |